VEGA

Plant-based Cookbook to Lose Weight and Live a Healthy Lifestyles

© Copyright 2019 by Joseph kagawa

All rights reserved.

This document is geared towards providing exact and reliable information with

regards to the topic and issue covered. The publication is sold with the idea that the

publisher is not required to render accounting, officially permitted, or otherwise,

qualified services. If advice is necessary, legal or professional, a practiced individual

in the profession should be ordered.

From a Declaration of Principles which was accepted and approved equally by a

Committee of the American Bar Association and a Committee of Publishers and

Associations.

In no way is it legal to reproduce, duplicate, or transmit any part of this document in

either electronic means or in printed format. Recording of this publication is strictly prohibited and any storage of this document is not allowed unless with written

permission from the publisher. All rights reserved.

The information provided herein is stated to be truthful and consistent, in that any

liability, in terms of inattention or otherwise, by any usage or abuse of any policies,

processes, or directions contained within is the solitary and utter responsibility of the

recipient reader. Under no circumstances will any legal responsibility or blame be

held against the publisher for any reparation, damages, or monetary loss due to the

information herein, either directly or indirectly.

Respective authors own all copyrights not held by the publisher.

The information herein is offered for informational purposes solely, and is universal

as so. The presentation of the information is without contract or any type of

guarantee assurance.

The trademarks that are used are without any consent,

and the publication of the

trademark is without permission or backing by the trademark owner. All trademarks

and brands within this book are for clarifying purposes only and are the owned by the

owners themselves, not affiliated with this document.

Disclaimer

All erudition contained in this book is given for informational and educational purposes only. The author is not in any way accountable for any results or outcomes that emanate from using this material. Constructive attempts have been made to provide information that is both accurate and effective, but the author is not bound for the accuracy or use/misuse of this information.

Foreword

First, I will like to thank you for taking the first step of trusting me and deciding to purchase/read this life-transforming eBook. Thanks for spending your time and resources on this material.

I can assure you of exact results if you will diligently follow the exact blueprint, I lay bare in the information manual you are currently reading. It has transformed lives, and I strongly believe it will equally transform your own life too.

All the information I presented in this Do It Yourself piece is easy to digest and practice.

Table of Contents

INTRODUCTION TO VEGAN DIET 3

CHAPTER ONE 12

PLANT-BASED NUTRITION IN A NUTSHELL 12

Shifting To Plant-Based Eating Is Not As Difficult As You Think 13

Top Ten Advantages of a Plant Based Diet 14

Why Trainers Do Greatest Having a Plant Based Diet 15

Energizing Up Using Plant-Based Proteins 17

Outfitting Your Internal Herbivore 21

Observing A Plant Based Diet Can Be Easy With Home Gardens 26

CHAPTER TWO 29

YOUR PLANT BASED KITCHEN 29

Natural Herbal Plants For Better Health 34

CHAPTER THREE 39

4 WEAK MEAL PLAN 39

Veggie lover shopping list 39

Test supper plan 43

7-Day Vegan Meal Plan: 1,200 Calories 45

CHAPTER FOUR 51

MORNING RECIPES 51

CHAPTER FIVE 73

LUNCH RECIPES 73

CHAPTER 100

SIX DINNER RECIPES 100

CONCLUSION 108

INTRODUCTION TO VEGAN DIET

The veggie enthusiast diet is known for is medical benefits, and especially - weight loss. Various individuals have undergone the veggie lover diet for the only reason to get fit, and have predominant with respect to doing such. If that you're interested in finding a solid and secure eating routine for more healthy and are considering the vegetarian diet, then you need to ask yourself: is it secure? Might it be astute? Is it possible?

Is it secure?

In the event that you encounter the vegetarian diet in an honest, well-arranged manner, you may be sure that it's equally secure and strong. You need to ensure that you're ingesting a broad selection of nourishments always to ensure that you're accepting perfect sustenance - nevertheless hello, you need to get this done on any eating regime. If you somehow were able to drop back on eating veggie enthusiast low excellent nourishment all the time, your health would obviously endure.

Veggie lover low-quality nourishment comprises packaged crisps, chips that are hot, with no milk chocolate and parts of candies, alleged 'health bars' which are pressed with sugars and so on. Should you somehow be able to expend nourishments, as an instance, that all of the time and eat them rather than your proper suppers, you're damaging your body? Instead, you can choose to create your own vegetarian preparing strategies, by way of instance, without milk, low-sugar snacks, brownies, cakes, oat and nut cuts, so on., such as dates, dried organic goods, crisp all-natural goods, nuts, coconut oil, extra-virgin olive seeds, and oil. Experience your eating regimen in a judicious and continuous manner, and provide your body with the nutritional supplements that it requires.

Might it be astute?

In case you need to shed weight, the veggie lover diet is one of those good eating regimens which it is possible to adapt to perform as such. It's rash to choose a fad diet that's low in fat, saturated in leaves and supplements one feeling denied. It's possible to enjoy avocadoes, olive oil, seeds and nuts with this particular eating regimen - maybe not at all like most injury abstains from food now. You may likewise appreciate a range of gourmet, strong cooking so that you won't need to feel refused. By producing your own heavenly and strong veggie fan heating plans, you're guaranteeing you will stay happy and chemical with this eating regimen, instead of frustrated and grumpy.

So if the veggie lover diet offers you a great deal of sound nutritional supplements, provides your body sufficient sound fats and does not leave you feeling denied, alright say it is wise or indiscreet to drift down this pathway? I'd say it is savvy.

Is it sensible?

There are some long drag veggie fans who've been on the vegetarian diet as long as they can recall or for quite a very long moment. These people are always lean and thin and possess a solid, shiny composition along with also a get-up-and-go that most are desirous of. Not at all like injury eats, this eating routine is reasonable. Why? You won't feel denied since there are a lot of yummy choices to consume. You're able to enjoy a broad range of beautiful veggie-lover heating programs or dinner programs, which can be anything but hard to find in books, on the internet, or by vegetarian formula electronic publications. The health care benefits of the eating regimen can permit you to understand it is well-worth neglecting meat and meat products. Several have completed as such and therefore are moving to do so now. Could this be you?

Weight loss on the vegetarian diet is sheltered, educated and economical. So perhaps it's now a chance to drop the entirety of your injury diet musings and thoughts, and select rather a solid, veggie enthusiast way of life which can leave your life components happy, strong and well-supported.

The talk of whether the vegetarian diet is unfortunate or sound is not new. The majority of people may say that an individual that embraces veganism will probably be inadequate in fundamental supplements found obviously in animal products, to be particular, animal-based protein. These individuals treasure the certainty that milk can keep their bones strong and red meat will provide standard protein to your own muscles.

Then again, there's a little minority of individuals (2 percent veggie lover and 5 percent vegetarian) who provide credit into the plant-based eating regimen relieving their real health problems, enabling them to get rid of overabundance weight, clearing their skin up and sensitivities, also providing them an astonishing pizzazz.

So determined by those two contrasts in evaluations, how could one determine whether the veggie lover diet is undesirable or solid? Everything boils down to, not things 'conclusion,' nevertheless instead, on powerful actualities, evidence, contextual investigations and fair accounts of real people.

Meat eaters vs. Veggie eaters

Different investigations demonstrate that drinkers of reddish meat are certain to kick the bucket rashly compared to people who eat nearly no red meat. 1 us-based evaluation of 120,000 people verified that drinkers of reddish meat are 20 percent bound to pass more young. The people who ate ready meats regularly supported this abrupt passing speed to a further 20% greater.

Then again, Michael f. Roizen, MD, infers the people who switch from eating meat things to veggie enthusiast nourishments could without a lot of stretches include at any speed 13 years into their life. Why? Veggie fans eat less animal cholesterol and fat, while vegetarians devour no monster cholesterol or fat. Educator t. Colin. Campbell (raised on a dairy product) closes out of his evaluation research program meat and with no dairy diet may both prevent and turn about 70-80percent of disease!

Weight reduction proof

Actuality: most milk and meat things are high in calorie and fat content. As an example, 100g of hens comprises around 294 calories and 21g of fat (9% fat) whereas 100g of cooked legumes comprise only 128 calories and 6.5g of fat (0.8g immersed). Sheep contains 0g dietary fiber, while 100g of lentils comprises 7.5grams dietary fiber. Fiber makes you feel more complete for longer.

Proof:

Angela stokes (aka'veggie fan raw food goddess') dropped over 154lbs (70kg) about the vegetarian primitive nourishment diet. This astonishing lady, once tremendously plump, supports her weight reduction and recently found energy into the veggie lover crude nourishment diet and won't return into the conventional American way of eating! Why? The health care benefits of the veggie lover diet (particularly weight loss for Angela's situation) are too amazing to consider giving up. Angela received primitive veganism medium-term and hasn't believed back since.

Physical gains

Over and over, those who get veganism declare their skin clears up (skin eczema, inflammation, etc), their eyes turn into white, their hair becoming thicker and much more valuable, their claws become more relaxed, their energy levels soar as well as their sensitivities clean up. Is the sound too good to even consider being try, is not that so?

These astonishing health tributes may be ascribed to the high nutrient and nutritional content utilized in sharp goods of their soil, seeds and nuts, vegetables and legumes, lush greens and whole-grain nourishments. The American dietetic association inferred a well-arranged veggie enthusiast or vegetarian diet is with no doubt'healthfully satisfactory,' and can provide various medical benefits and cure or counteract specific infections. Really well-arranged' veggie enthusiast diet will provide you a liberal measure of basic minerals and nutrients, so with no doubt, one's health will improve.

The veggie enthusiast's way of existence is both testing and fulfilling concurrently. Those new to the veggie lover diet should have an intensive understanding and data on this manner of life together produce the advancement of turning out to become vegetarian as straightforward as may reasonably be anticipated. This will ensure you will know exactly what is in store, also will aid you in coping with and see some issues that may arise. The corresponding 3 hints are, especially for its apprentice vegetarian. They'll help you with knowing how to commence a veggie fan diet efficiently. As it had been, the means in which to ensure going great!

Hint # 1 - know in advance that the benefits and challenges

The compensating section of this vegetarian diet comprises astounding health and mental benefits such as weight loss, clear skin, fewer sensitivities, an inversion or reduction of incessant illness, a more gradual aging process, cerebral stability and joy, and capability to heart and concentrate much better. The challenging view contains how loved ones will react initially and long haul, the longings that you'll grow (especially toward the start of the eating regime to your fledgling vegetarian), the evaluation of eating out, triggering detox episodes, and feeling as somewhat of a burden when individuals should plan distinguishing nourishment just for you.

Research others that have gone the veggie enthusiast diet and determine what they have struck. What exactly did they say was the most analyzing angle? Can it make easier for them? Likewise, find out what benefits and benefits they struck. You are going to find on your examination that many societies will agree the prizes by a large margin exceed any issues or impediments experienced about the veggie enthusiast lifestyle!

Hint # 2 - collect and find great vegan recipes

This is among the very significant tips for progressing into the veggie lover diet. It's essential for every student veggie lover to start their diet entirely organized, i.e., with a great deal of exceptional vegetarian strategies. Possessing a substantial measure of programs accumulated will guarantee that the corresponding:

1. This you can plan something quick and easy once you're feeling worn out or busy

2. Will spare you the annoyance of pursuing veggie enthusiast plans whenever you're basically not in the character.

3. At the stage when you're longing for a candy treat, you are able to visit your formulation assortment and warmth your sound cut or cake, rather than going off your eating routine or ingesting package vegetarian bad nourishment.

Discover your veggie fan plans online by way of websites, sites, you-tube, or simply by obtaining a vegetarian formula electronic publication (notice: veggie-lover formulation electronic publications contain substantial quantities of flavorful plans produced by skillful veggie-lover culinary specialists). You can purchase a veggie-lover formula cookbook in the local book store, yet that is generally the most costly choice. The conclusion of where you receive your programs would be yours.

Hint # 3 - permit family, friends, and co-workers know

It's essential to advise dear companions, family as well as collaborators that you're embracing a veggie enthusiast lifestyle. This may fill as insurance for you and will make your shift to the vegetarian diet as calm as can be expected under the conditions. In what capacity? Listed below are a couple of scenarios that you'll be protected from:

1. At the stage when companies or family to see you, they will certainly understand what you're eating vegetarian only nutrition and will stop from bringing cakes or bread rolls which you can not consume. Truth be told they will most likely have gone into the problem of picking a veggie-lover treat in the supermarket - only to impart to you!

2. You'll be spared by a fantastic deal of questions and cross-examinations in bistros and cafés, ever since your companions have only been educated concerning your selection (and probably, to a massive level, your own cross-examination will as of today be over!!!)

3. In get-togethers, end of the year festivities, and parties, everything considered, the host will ensure that there's some nourishment there which you may eat. There is nothing more dreadful than going to a gathering rather than having the choice to eat some of the nutrition (been there, done that. I don't imply that

you place yourself in this circumstance).

8 measures from the transition to the vegan diet: how to begin a vegan diet

For those individuals that are new into the veggie lover diet, the notion of a sudden refraining from meat and dairy products could be wholly alarming. In the current society, the majority of men and women combine meat, eggs, and legumes into a massive degree of everyday nourishment consumption. This way, in case it is your craving to adopt the vegetarian diet, and you're overpowered at deserting your favorite nourishments medium-term, you should rather create a gradual improvement to the veggie lover diet plan. The corresponding 8 phases disclose how to start a veggie fan diet together with advancement!

The gradual transition for your beginner vegan:

Period 1: remove red meat

The first step should be quite simple. Cut out all sheep, hamburger, pork and other red meat out of your eating regime, yet allow to eat white meat (poultry, fish, and fish). Likewise know you could buy sans meat"bacon" and veggie enthusiast"mince" from many markets and health stores. At the stage when you're starting to feel good not eating red meat, then proceed to the subsequent phase.

Stage 2: remove chicken

Only consume fish and fish things for some time, and steer clear of each other meat such as chicken. Become acclimated to becoming prepared with no meat, and start asking about formula ideas for vegetarian suppers.

Phase 3: remove fish and seafood

Now you'll be going totally veggie enthusiast. Instead of eating fish and meat, your protein will currently be originating from veggies (chickpeas, lentils, black beans and so forth.), whole grains, broccoli, cabbage enthusiast" patties," vegan" mince," along with other sans meat products, as an instance, vegetarian"bacon" bear in mind that nowadays it's possible to find a massive number of vegan nourishments on the marketplace. Become more familiar with all the brands and items available. Furthermore, do not fear tofu, it very well might be incredibly elastic and heavenly whenever cooked suitably. It may retain the sorts of distinct nourishments and tastes it is cooked/marinated together, so find the way to cook it so it is going to taste lovely!

Stage 4: remove cheese

This is the principal stage of this advancement from veggie enthusiasts to vegetarians. For your apprentice veggie-lover, the notion of surrendering cheddar things may seem to be somewhat down-gladdening, because many societies love cheddar always: on their own pasta, inside their dishes of mixed greens, in their own sandwiches, even in their sauces... That the rundown continues! Be as it might, on the off possibility you want to in the very long term get the many astonishing wellbeing benefits of this vegetarian diet - you need to kill cheddar out of your eating regime. In the event, this is difficult for you (probably), in that point get some of the false cheeses (veggie enthusiasts) from the local store.

Stage 5: remove eggs

This is additionally troublesome progress for a few, however, know that eggs are a monster thing, and this manner depriving them is an unquestionable requirement for those people who would like to go on the veggie lover diet. It's possible to earn numerous yummy counterfeit egg dishes with tofu (e.g.: lettuce"fried eggs"), and also in case you pursue an amazing formulation and receive the tastes right - you probably won't overlook your eggs!

Period 6: remove butter and cream

You have currently murdered all of your strong creature nourishments out of your eating regimen. The subsequent prescribed phase on your improvement to veggie enthusiast would be to go without cream and margarine, and all things comprising both of these ingredients. You are able to use numerous distinct fats and oils instead, by way of instance, olive oil, coconut oil, and veggie enthusiast margarine. You ought to cook the great majority of your veggie enthusiast desserts today because most snacks and cakes at bistros and shops include eggs and margarine.

Period 7: remove the milk

This should not be too hard, because there are a lot of veggie enthusiast options to drain nowadays. You are able to consume soy milk, rice milk, coconut milk, and so forth. You are able to cook or prepare these bowls of milk, eat them along with your oat, or only drink them by a glass!

Period 8: obtain some vegan recipes

As you are 100% veggie fan, as well as the entirety of your suppers beginning now and in the near future will be vegetarian, then you need to assemble a whole lot of tasty vegetarian strategies! You are able to find some extraordinary programs online on websites, internet journals, or by getting a professional veggie enthusiast formula electronic publication. Your formulation assortment should include a diverse scope of programs, such as veggie enthusiast suppers, snacks, suppers, morning meals, cakes, cuts, snacks, pastries, and quick dinners.

Concerning the vegan diet and its health benefits

Hardly any Americans understand exactly what a veggie-lover diet is, or what it may mean for their health. Instead of an eating regimen rich in foods increased from the floor, the typical American eating pattern is overpowering in animal grains, meats, and milk. Together these lines of ingestion were deteriorating with each era. As this particular angle, so do lots of individuals' waistlines. Eating a veggie-lover diet instead is a strong alternative option. Irrespective of whether you consume a vegetarian diet for a short span, or go to get a life, veganism may be a remunerating method of lifestyle change.

Get thinner, enjoy more vitality, and texture amazing by rolling out that the addition to veganism.

What's veganism?

Veganism is a type of vegetarianism that's somewhat increasingly limited. Even though a veggie-lover will not eat beef, some nevertheless enjoy eggs, milk, nectar, and other animal things. Vegetarians, then again, eliminate each and every animal item imaginable. Many even detract from sporting calfskin and fleece in light of how these are animal things. Vegetarians will need to always be watchful for animal-based nutrition additional substances. 1 regular model is reddish nourishment shade, which can be produced utilizing a sort of germs.

Is veganism difficult to follow from the start, it is apparently quite difficult to pursue a vegetarian diet. Creature items are around, in the gelatin to chocolate. Quite a few nourishments you wouldn't expect to possess monster products, do. In some specific portions of the planet, choosing to consume a vegetarian diet might be incredibly difficult to do. Be as it might, for fantastic many individuals in u.s. there's a plenitude of nutrition choices in case you understand where to search. Wellbeing nourishment shops and claim to popularity stores are certain to convey veggie enthusiast nourishment that normal standard food thing chains. Anyhow some larger chains, as an instance, Walmart, are beginning to convey veggie fan and vegetarian options.

Small, nearby markets often have an adequate selection of snappy nourishment items that are veggie enthusiast benevolent. Otherwise, they may be even more neighborly towards creating these decisions available to tackle nearby troubles. When going out to eat, a couple of cooking styles are more capable of providing veggie enthusiast choices. Spanish, both south and central

America, and a few Asian nourishments have incredible vegetarian options. What's more, fortunately, more veggie enthusiast benevolent eateries are opening up the country over daily.

On the off chance that wants be, it is possible to generally request the gourmet pro hold the animal items for your own dish. Vegetarian snacks are not anything but hard to find. Crisp foods rose from the earth, alongside seeds and nuts, are all sound bites that comprise absolutely no animal items.

Try a lot of cashews, a crisp organic merchandise plate of mixed greens, along with even a square of chocolate to get a fundamental veggie enthusiast nibble.

Can it be delicious?

You will find veggie enthusiast dishes all around the world, dishes a fantastic a lot of folks don't know are vegetarian. Hummus, singed okra, portions of mixed greens, chocolate. Heaps of items that people appreciate regularly don't have any animal items in any way.

Where the American eating routine centers for the most part about meat and animal fats, appearing out our culture we could find a wide mixture of celestial nourishments to love. Since the interest grows, numerous nutrition organizations are now offering vegetarian alternatives which are equally as tasty as the food resources they supplant. From vegetarian adaptations of bacon, hotdog, hamburgers, and floor hamburger, you will find extraordinary choices for people intrigued by means of a veggie enthusiast diet but not yet ready to bid farewell to meat.

Vegetarians do not need to give their candy choices either. Cakes, snacks, frozen yogurts, and much more would be able to be produced without eggs and milk, and they're equally as yummy as the common variations. Try a slice of veggie enthusiast crusty fruit-filled cure, conquer with vegetarian frozen yogurt generated using coconut milk. Quite a few people discover that since they acclimate to a veggie lover diet, their own sense of flavor never requires aggressively improved nourishments. Matters can taste candy with sugar that making pastries somewhat better.

As their frameworks clean out the crap developed, they could prove to become touchy to what they consume.

Is veganism safe?

An honest vegetarian diet may be mind-blowing for your own wellbeing. Evidently, the puzzle is maintaining it corrected. An eating pattern of just veggie-lover treats, whilst vegetarian, wouldn't be strong by any stretch of the imagination. Sticking to some reasonable eating routine and ensuring to consume nourishments with some restraint is going to help you with being more valuable and becoming thinner. Really, even people that are as of today in a solid weight land will feel much better if their own body flushes the animal things out.

Benefits of a vegan diet and the human body was designed to be performed

The human body wasn't intended to consume meat and not milk, but rather for a plant amicable veggie enthusiast diet. We've got over 30 dissimilarities with carnivores, which can be likenesses we discuss with herbivores about our strategy. For example, our gut-associated tract is a very long plant encouraging you. A real flesh-eater includes a brief stomach associated tract and beef is completed in 3-7 hours. This will not allow parasites to bring forth. In individuals it takes three days to process beef, giving it ample moment for parasites to bring forth. That's a significant bit of the estimated 90 percent of people have parasites!

Anyway, we've got nails rather than pins, varied gut corrosiveness, spit, and our teeth arrangement is similar to herbivores and surely not a carnivore. It is in our impulses not to eat meat too. For example, on the off likelihood that you just saw a deceased bovine on the bud, you would not start salivating or will need to consume it like this. A real meat-eater would consume off. The major way you'd need it's if that you cooked it, in crops oils, and prepared it using herbs, etc. This is also since you've grown up eating beef so have been used to it. Be as it may, the body wasn't meant for meat, nevertheless instead a veggie fan diet.

Meat is full of saturated fats and less pristine as plants. Also, if your beef is not organic, grass-encouraged, and unfenced, you need to handle improvement hormones, anti-toxins, and steroids. All of that develops you and causes you to increasingly impervious to antimicrobials. Additionally any uneasiness, also anxiety the monster underwent in its own life made artificial reactions within the body, by way of instance, enlarged levels of cortisol and adrenaline, which you have it, wind up in you. No major surprise such enormous numbers of people are mad and once we believe veggie fans we believe smooth, relaxed people. Additionally, meat is indeed hard to process. Assimilation takes up the larger portion of your energy for the day. If that you're processing mangoes versus beef, that do you think is more faithfully on the human body and provides you more energy to do everything you need to do?

Additional dairy is extremely alarming. It is the absolute most noticeably dreadful everything being equivalent. We take milk, normally from an abused bovine who's given steroids, hormones, and antimicrobials, and cook it. Any nutritional supplements in the milk are presently gone, in fact, the milk is still acidic. We at the point brace the milk together with calcium and nutrients, however, it's not really the real article. At the stage when it pops up on your body it's acidic to the stage your body should use its magnesium and calcium save simply to kill the causticity. So's right, milk actually exhausts your assortment of calcium. You've lately been dissipated of possibly the most wonderful dream within recent memory. Additionally milk is similarly full of malodorous fats also leaves you to put on fat efficiently. Think about what that milk has been intended for, baby dairy animals. That kid cow develops a lot of pounds in its first season only off this milk.

So you need to figure, where do i get my protein, calcium, and b12 out of a veggie lover daily diet? You may find a great deal of protein in lush greens, nuts, legumes, sea green expansion, as well as sprouts. You merely want 5 to 10 percent protein in one single diet to build all of the muscle you desire and desire. According to the world health institution you simply need 5 percent protein and there's never been an example of protein deficiency in most of medicinal composing. Long amounts of individual and research experience have persuaded this whole protein publicity is a marketing methodology from the meat industry. I consume 5 percent of the calories as protein and don't have any difficulty building muscle. In fact, since my nourishment is primitive and aren't denatured and even more dominant, I have a much ton easier timekeeping and building muscle onto a veggie fan diet.

Calcium can be found in bounty in its crude and unbelievable arrangement in lush green vegetables. 1 pound of lush greens, by way of instance, spinach or kale will provide you 100% of your RDA requirements for your day. B12 is genuinely a nutrient that's found in organic soil. In the event, you merely leave some of that nutrient abundant all-natural soil in your veggies you may get your b12. Whatever the situation, on the off possibility that you can not stay to do so, it's possible to normally improve. On the other hand, the veggie enthusiast diet really is great and ideal. An adequate veggie enthusiast diet has all of your nutritional supplement prerequisites and is pristine and ideal for the plant's nicely disposed body.

So by the day's conclusion, for that which reason would you need to consume a solid veggie enthusiast diet? After all, I will provide you a bit of executioner, accurate, and astonishing explanations. A veggie enthusiast diet, especially high is primitive nourishments, will provide you vitality. This is about the grounds that a top or complete primitive veggie enthusiast diet is rich in nutritional supplements, easy to process, and mild. Who has to be worn out during the day? Vitality is enjoyable and makes everything a lot more energizing. This is about the grounds that you're getting supplements rather than spending such a great quantity of your energy processing substantial nourishments which are often piled with toxins.

Additionally, you'll receive more fit. A veggie enthusiast diet is high in fiber, which keeps you complete, and nutritional supplements so that you do not eat and eat and eat. Additionally, plants are v diversely from the human body because we have been intended to get a plant cordial veggie enthusiast diet. They move out and in and are used for energy and nutritional supplements. At the stage once we eat animal items or the most up to date gmo chemical and toxins, the body does not have any idea how to handle them so that they often get put away as fat, especially around the midriff! How frequently do you see someone on a veggie lover diet who's obese?

Various motives to select a vegetarian diet are you'll slow aging. Really! The way you age is usually heavily influenced by you personally, and hereditary attributes have a small effect, however not every last piece of it. The great majority of the best way to age is due to your eating routine, the way you deal with yourself through exercise, hydration, rest, and the way you oversee anxiety. You're in control and it's possible to be a sexy grandma at 70 such as Annette Larkins and lots of other sexy senior citizens on a full or high primitive veggie enthusiast diet. A vegetarian diet, certain high in crude products of this soil has lots of enemies and supplements of oxidants. Enemies of oxidants combat free radical harm and assist moderate maturing. I really don't think about you personally, yet I do not expect to get old and am thankful for the primitive vegetarian diet for earning that possible.

Chapter one

Plant-based nutrition in a nutshell

With the importance of action and sustenance to maintain up perfect wellbeing to fend off the specialist, a significant lot of us consume what affects our taste buds nevertheless don't have the very best possible nourishment we need for our own bodies to perform at it's fullest capacity.

Regardless, imagine a situation where there was a way to check into your hereditary attributes and survey exactly what nutritional supplements your body is lacking. At the stage, in the aftermath of surveying your healthful lacks envision a situation where there existed this approach to produce nourishing enhancements which make up to your specific inadequacies throughout your one of a type DNA constitute.

I have uplifting news for you. Ever since without precedent for background scientists have completed the genome project and are now prepared to check into our hereditary makeup, create a DNA file, at the point make an outstanding mixture of whole nutrition, organics, superb all-natural solution, plant established sustenance nutritional supplements which are deductively proven to have any type of influence in health and nutrition determined by your one of a sort unique DNA.

In August 2008, Genewize life sciences brought to market the life map nutrition strategy as an accomplishment in science and have obtained the health and wellness sector by storm. Genewize life map nutrition strategy is best accounted for by different happy shoppers to provide more energy, perseverance, fixation, better rest, and also the assistance of joint distress, migraines, reduced heartbeat and a huge group of additional health-related ways. The instances of agreeing with regard to that which works for your personal wellbeing needs really are a relic of yesteryear. "why consider if you're able to be researched?" that's a boisterous spoken announcement pertaining to the all-new DNA established sustenance framework. Now, like never before are shoppers concurring that one size doe's not fit all with respect to nourishing enhancements.

Genewize LifeMap nutrition strategy is especially proposed and hereditarily coordinated for a modified sustenance frame based in the one of a type DNA. Each recipe is really created from a capacity of 120 ingredients and over 577,000 varieties. Everything starts with the client obtaining a self-managed cookie package through the post office, so in the point swabbing the inner cheek zone, and placing the swabs to the prepaid postage envelope that's bar code to your safety, at the point email back into Genewize life sciences laboratory to be assessed. Within 4 per month and a half, you'll find a replica of your DNA solid maturing report, a rundown of the ingredients on your recipe, and also a multi-month supply of your modified DNA established nutritional enhancements delivered to your entryway measure and always from there on auto-ship.

Similarly, as with every new logical accomplishment, there's always a little number of people who are devotees. What is more, this one is not a particular case in the standard. Many doubt that science has come this way while some take the negative path free of evaluation by any stretch of the imagination. Then again, many are likely into the life map nutrition strategy as an option to drugs and also as an aversion plan from some health-related sicknesses regularly surfacing in almost any instance.

Shifting To Plant-Based Eating Is Not As Difficult As You Think

A solid plant-based eating regimen is not generally such not exactly the same as a strong omnivorous eating regimen. In the event you are contemplating switching to a plant-based eating regime or having to combine more plant-based nourishment in your sustenance, it is a good deal easier than you might suspect.

A good eating routine, Irrespective of whether you consume only plants or combine plants, contains a solid accentuation on organic products, veggies, seeds, nuts, whole grains, legumes, and veggies. Really, even the people who call themselves veggie fans or drinkers can eat undesirable by not choosing the best crops to consume. For example, pizza and frozen yogurt (for the people who eat milk) are veggie enthusiast nourishments, nevertheless, they aren't favorable choices. Organizing your own sustenance suitably is important, along with the assumption of this should connect with whole characteristic nourishments.

The largest contrast between an omnivorous eating regular (one which includes meat) plus also a plant-based eating routine is where your protein is coming from. Aside from that, 80 percent of this eating regimen is going to be equal (because that's the thing that everyone ought to focus on). Quite a few people eat meat 2-3 times every day. The ideal place to start would be to control your beef use to 2-3 times per week.

The best dream of eating plant-based eating regularly is that you don't get sufficient protein as you aren't eating beef. There are a whole lot of approaches to receive incredible protein resources out of plant-based nourishments. The one nourishment which has the maximum protein you may find is tempeh (soy protein). One cup of tempeh has up to 41 g of protein, even more than you may frequently discover at a beef. One cup of legumes has up to 18 grams of protein, kidney beans consumed up to 13 g. Chickpeas are just another, which consume up to 12 g in one cup. Nuts are similarly an extraordinary choice. A quarter cup of almonds consume up to 8 grams of protein; per quarter cup of sunflower seeds contains 6 grams of protein. You may be surprised to discover that broccoli has protein in it! 1 cup of cooked broccoli contains four grams of protein.

Protein is in virtually anything that's whole regular nourishment. Quite a few people just include things like an animal protein within their own protein g, but you really can get more protein from a plant-based eating regimen than you can use a meat-based eating regime. Enhancements are also accessible in powder arrangement where you are able to add your own protein into something such as a smoothie. Some extraordinary ones to start trying are dark colored rice and berry protein.

Get Health using a Plant-Based Diet

Imagine a situation where straightforward change could set you on a method to enhance health. What is more, envision a situation where change may even save you out of corpulence, coronary disease, and cancerous growth. You have the capacity to change your life by maintaining a plant established eating regular - no doubts concerning it.

While many omnivores feel a feast without meat only does not feel like a supper, the veggie enthusiast and vegetarian plant established manner of life are growing in ubiquity in any case - and everything considered. A plant established eating regimen goes from animal-based nourishments like beef, eggs, and milk, and consolidates more organic solution, vegetables, vegetables, and grains. The meat and milk you consume the less fat you consume in. This goes much with respect to maintaining up audio fat and cholesterol levels.

If you're wondering whether you should appraise a plant established eating regimen, think about the very best five benefits recorded under. Bear in mind you don't have to dip to an all-out veggie enthusiast diet or vegetarian diet. Simply limiting your entrance of poultry, meat, and milk, and enlarging vegetables, leafy foods may perform ponders to your health.

Top Ten Advantages of a Plant Based Diet

1.) Lower Cholesterol

Practicing environmental consciousness can significantly reduce the amount of LDL cholesterol in your bloodstream - the horrible kind that may prompt coronary stroke and disease. Maintain a strategic space from dispersing, cut fatty meats out and choose on healthful nourishments. Dairy and monster things are piled with fat and don't have any fiber. Plant-based nourishments include no cholesterol in any way. This implies vegetarian nutrition is significantly improved for your own heart and your health. It has been shown through a continuous report from St. Michael's Hospital in Toronto, which discovered a low-carb plant established eating regimen could reduce LDL cholesterol by 28 percent.

2.) Reduce Blood Pressure

At the stage when you eat fatty meat and dairy products, the consequences of your blood flow, putting more fat on the veins. A plant established eating routine tops off you with vegetables and organic solution, which can be full of potassium. The greater entrance of potassium adjusts blood depth. This is why veggie lovers and vegetarians will generally have reduced paces of hypertension, "the silent executioner," according to observational investigations dispersed in the Nutrition Review.

3.) Avoid Cancer

High-fat weight management programs have been linked to greater paces of cancerous growth. Truth be told the Physicians Committee for Responsible Medicine's Cancer Project revealed vegans to be 40 percent less likely to make disease compared to meat-eaters. The meat will generally be high in saturated fat and low in fiber. Fiber presumes an integral role in maintaining your gut-related frame sound and perfect, evacuating cancerous growth-inducing combinations until they could make damage. A veggie enthusiast vegetarian and diet are high in fiber, low in immersed and trans-fats and generally include more natural solution, vegetables as well as other disease-preventing phytochemicals.

4.) Prevent Cardiovascular Disease

The American Heart Association States 83 million Americans have some form of cardiovascular disease, and a substantial bunch of the risk variables, as an instance, stoutness, are in unsurpassed highs. Be as it may, you reduce your own threat. Studies have found that a moderate, low carb, plant established eating regimen might help reduce cholesterol, add to fat reduction and reduced circulatory strain. All of which contribute to heart problems.

5.) Keep Healthy Weight and Fitness

The individuals who pursue a Plant established, veggie enthusiast or vegetarian diet for the most part expend fewer calories and also have lower body heaps compared to people who don't, in accordance with the Mayo Clinic. Whatever the circumstance, a plant established eating regimen does not guarantee weight loss. You will have to keep your entrance of greasy and desserts nourishments low, select whole grains, consume a range of foods grown in the floor, and select without low-fat and fat dairy products. Likewise recollect that cooking procedure assesses. Steam, bubble, dinner or grill rather than singing. Your new diet may also offer you re-established energy for bodily exercise.

Step-by-step directions to Transition into a Plant-Based Diet

Beside basically keeping a Strategic space from beef, there are strategies to ease the change to some fundamentally plant established eating regimen. Increment the number of grain foods grown on the floor in the plate step by step till the meat is the tiniest piece of your dinner. An internet vegetarian conveyance management can produce the process easy.

Why Trainers Do Greatest Having a Plant-Based Diet

We've got the living arrangements of a plant-eater. We do not have the pins, teeth, digestive organs of a meat-eater. We do not possess the blinding speed, the overwhelming touchiness, or some of the distinct capacities necessary to murder and catch a victim. Our mouth does not water seeing a bull. The vision of guys, women, and kids lounging around a recently executed body, with a fantastic time its usage violence is an abomination. We use other people to perform our slaughtering to us in the pressing home, abattoirs to dismantle the entire body, and butchers to finish the activity. As soon as we see and purchase our beef, cut into small fragments and all washed of violence, it's not ever again jaded as the joyous animal it might have been.

Our structure underpins our use of crops. We consume products of the dirt vegetables exceptionally well while we struggle to process beef, which often breaks down until it digests. Our fat and protein requirements are uncommonly reduced while our dependence on starches is likewise large, a percentage which most supports crops. Fiber, found in abundance in foods rose from the earth, suits us nicely, nevertheless meat gives not one of the important nutritional supplements. Our faculties have a fantastic time the eyesight, smell, and flavor of the pure solution, practically that are ergonomically meant to fit into our palms, although it's the utter magnificence of seeing living creatures in real life which we seem to love most.

With regards to athletic Implementation, which nourishments best aid the rival in their assignment for incidence on the area? Quite a few competitors have conveyed the belief which they're on any occasion, prepared to place their own health apart because they continued searching for fame. Which diet will best serve the competition? Is nutrition a figure deserving of the idea that this respect?

From the Sixties, sustenance for competitions undergone a substantial upheaval. Meat, and lots of it, was the eating regime of choice for competitions up till that moment. A long-separation sprinter discovered he could enhance his display be eating more notable quantities of boring nourishment than he had been used to and an eating regular unrest for competitions started. The meat-based pre-game feast has been supplanted by the poorly recognized and in the very long-term vulnerable notion of carbo-stacking. A couple of competitions guessed that if marginally was good, increasingly ought to be greater, and discovered, to their own insecurities, that exhibit actually enhanced when normally speaking sugar usage increased.

The investigators had each one of that the clarifications significant to legitimize this development. They indicated that a low-carb, low-protein (when compared with the Normal Westernized Diet) diet which has been prevailed via starches, for its corresponding reasons:

1. As fat or protein entrance increases, sugar ingestion must rust. Sugars are the crucial fuel hotspot for competitions, so ingesting an overabundance of proteins or fats suggests eating inadequately of starches, the result being diminished gas openness to the competitor. 2. Protein entrance in the teens or more notable, as a part of all calories out, has been looked to stress both the liver and kidneys, organs which are of today under amazing worry due to the requests of exceptional athletic undertakings. 3. Fat entry into the teens and higher generally decreases the oxygen-conveying limitation of their blood. Take-up, transportation, and conveyance of the vital supplement are diminished in blood flow extent to an ascent in fat. 4. The capacity of this human body to send and communicate starches to fuel the muscles and unique cells is also diminished in reverse extent to an ascent in fat. 5. Abundance protein entrance slopes the competitor to induce cracks due to the high number of corrosive minerals inalienable in pertinacious nourishments, which, in order to be murdered, filter soluble minerals in the bones, which makes the bones flimsier.

The sugar anger had begun. Pasta, bread, pasta, rice, and corn turned into"hugely popular" since the nourishments of choice for competitions. Carbo-stacking turned to the norm. Tragically, physiologists across the world had only proven that the body doesn't have any capability to store either sugar or protein. "Utilitarian amounts" of each one of these clairaudients are located within the human body of course, and such as gas in your car's tank, the amount can rise or drop indoors foreordained criteria, nevertheless abundance beyond helpful points of confinement can not be placed away. Each overabundance calorie is set away as fat, whether or not they originate from carbohydrates, fats, or sugars. The thought of starch piling was shown for a legend, best-case scenario, manufacturing even from a bleak standpoint. All that had happened was that competitions that were accustomed to doing with reduced supplies of starch shown they performed when expending perfect quantities of the important yet frequently underestimated nutritional supplement. Plants had begun to catch in the eating regime of their competitor.

Three effects deserving of accepting Notice of occurred due to opponents expanding their usage of starches. To begin with, they have been now prepared to push more earnestly than any time due to just a small change in dietary plan that preferred plants over animals. This made a necessity for, and also the creation of, better hardware that has been designed for care for the enlarged concerns of more elevated degree displays. Innovation had its own day; using fiberglass supplanting aluminum, plaid supplanting soot, turf supplanting bud, hi-tech materials hammering onto the scene, lightweight stuff supplanting thicker ones, in most areas of effort. Tracks, pools, and even areas of "bud" obtained faster. Simultaneously, health hardware also improved radically. These components consolidated to deliver us competitions which may perform at more considerable amounts and also had the hardware to perform as such. The next important change was in teaching techniques. Inventiveness caught hold as competitors revealed they might violate each present document and mentors vie for further. New methods for pulling out the finest in each competitor were made. Sports mind mathematics, plyometrics, obstruction classes, and a vast range of planning aids came into usage.

From the late '90s, essentially all Genuine opponents were being subjected to this of late "elevated bar" of needs so far as their demonstration. Each of them approached the new invention. The arrival of this net made practically all instruction processes accessible to any person who desired them. There was just one "clear-cut advantage" abandoned, nutrition. Dietary change was coming to the front as the best single thing which a rival could do in order to put him/her over the wannabes. The point was set for crops to conquer the athletic world.

Energizing Up Using Plant-Based Proteins

Most meat-eating Americans have been Ingestion about 1.5-multiple situations the recommended dietary remittance for nourishment, which is good, then, really most of the extra protein is originating from animal items often high in carbs and ailing from the nourishing benefits which other plant-based proteins may give.

Protein may help control appetite, which is why it's crucial to have a protein supply with each dinner. If You're keen on enlarging your protein intake with plant-based nourishments, select food resources from this rundown:

• Beans, beans! Adzuki beans, dark beans, kidney beans, legumes - etc, are all full of protein.

• Ancient Grains such as quinoa, amaranth and grain

- Brown Rice, whole-grain bread and yogurt

- Nuts And seeds and their own spreads. Strive citrus spread, cashew vanilla and margarine spread for a change.

- Top Grain and yogurt using chia seeds or flaxseed dinner.

- Green Veggies: Edamame, spinach, peas, broccoli and kale

- Lentils

- Corn

Keep in mind that dairy products like Milk and milk are pressed with protein (and heaps of additional critical nutritional supplements) also. If that you would rather get milk optional, proceed with soymilk. Almond milk and almond milk are low in protein. Nourishment experts, founders, diet pros and physicians have their very own speculations with respect to sustenance. Cut out sugar cut fat... no pause, fat is excellent, eliminated gluten. New data, diet and studies publications spring up week by week with fresh ideas and"enchantment" eats fewer carbohydrates for us to pursue. However, one thing that ALL pros can urge is that we must consume MORE leafy foods. Everyone's health and prosperity can benefit by moving into some more plant-based eating regimes, so can character!

The Advantages of Plant-Based Protein Powder

Plant-based protein powders talk To a different mainstream pattern in nutrition. There are many motives behind this, nevertheless essentially one of them will be the obvious limits of whey protein along with the limited indicators of a significant number of the chief plant proteins. For vegetarians, these powders are essential to maintaining a good eating regimen. Whatever the inspiration for using rice, soy, pea or berry powder, then it's critical to understand the unmistakable factors of attention of every before heading out to purchase a particular enhancement. Each of these four is frequently persuasive swaps for whey protein, nevertheless a few of them deliver one of the type traits which might be the perfect suited for your own requirements.

Soy Protein Powder

Soy has for quite a while been understood from the "green" and solid living strategy as a persuasive swap for much additional protein source. The people that are lactose narrow-minded, are veggie fans or drinkers or possess hypersensitivities to certain grains, have gone into soy in order to find the basic protein their body needs. Among the benefits of soy powder really are it is low in fat, something not all protein powders may flaunt. What's more, soy powder is low in carbohydrates, while comprising numerous amino acids that are fundamental. A lot of examinations have suggested a constant eating regimen of soy protein to bring down "terrible" cholesterol. This might be a substantial element for particular folks hoping to bring their cholesterol down viably. For all intents and purposes, soy powder has been seen as incredibly mixable, suggesting it very well might be coordinated nicely with a broad range of teas, smoothies, and additional to preparing programs readily.

Rice Protein Powder

Rice protein powder is really a reasonably new growth to the plant established enhancement powder market. Among the chief benefits clients will generally note is that the distinctively lower retail price. This is about the grounds that rice is a by and large less expensive plant protein repairing. Though it does not have as a good deal of protein for each filling in as a part of distinct powders, rice is amazing since it communicates total amino acids which have never been split in the production process. Like soy protein, rice isn't anything but hard to process. Those who have experienced problems processing another dietary improvement might desire to try rice powder to decrease some of those indications. It's also another outstanding protein to blend in with drinks and preparing strategies.

Hemp Protein Powder

While hemp can invoke images of bud smoking young individuals, this plant established augmentation fills a completely distinct need when utilized as a protein supplement. Quite a few clients say that hemp powder includes a perceptibly preferable flavor over some of the different other choices. While this shouldn't be the principal aspect to consider it can have an impact when each other variable is equal. Hemp protein is a whole nourishment supply, rich in fat, no matter how the fantastic type of fat. The large fat levels could be a mood killer for a few prospective customers, but it's essential to produce eligibility among good and fats that are awful. Hemp is similarly extremely high in amino acids and other hard to acquire nutritional supplements, by way of instance, iron, zinc, and calcium.

Pea Protein Powder

Pea powder might seem to be a Far-fetched wellspring of nourishment, however the split pea was known for its own protein packaged nurturing essentialness for a long time. Notwithstanding being greatly rancid and normally mild, pea protein was shown not only to bring down heartbeat yet to boost kidney function also. The increased portion of the company protein powders comprises more than 25 g of protein for every single scoop that's extensively greater than a number of rice and soy powders. Weight lifters also point to the manner that pea protein contains over 5 g of BCAAs which hastens muscle building.

These plant-based improvements are incredibly successful, yet often go undetected for the profoundly firm whey powder. Truly these protein powders are likewise as persuasive as whey protein powder. While they're amazing for veggie fans and people who have hypersensitivities, plant-based proteins are a perfect option for many intents and purposes any person in almost any circumstance.

What do Mike Tyson, Bill Ford (obviously THE auto company), Steve Wynn of Wynn Resorts, Russell Simmons, and former president Bill Clinton all discuss for all intents and purpose? Sounds like the beginning of a terrible joke, right? After all, on the off possibility that you guessed that they all eat and rally to get the benefits of a vegetarian eating regime, you would be right.

(On the off Possibility that you Did not figure that, do not worry, you do not lose any targets here...)

Certainly, you have noticed that Diets similar to this are as of today all of the rave and the way VIPs seem to have on board with all the temporary trend right and left. Be as it may, what's all of the buzzes really about? Can there be anything behind the advertising, or is it a prevailing fad diet restricted to the planet's élite? All the more importantly, what could this be in a position to sort of diet achieve to our weight reduction goals as our overall wellbeing and prosperity?

Check Out "The Meat" Of A Plant-Based Diet

Much the same as it seems, the Saying "plant-based eating regular" alludes to some type of diet reliant on plant nourishments (frequently of this crisp assortment however a number of the time ready plant nourishments are integrated too) and recalls reducing hard for animal items.

Be as it may, you will find an Expansive range of "plant-eaters" out there scavenging our grocery shops, and each of these herbivore personalities eats as signaled by several criteria, contingent upon their health objectives and also eating methods of justification.

As an example, veganism is a serious Adaptation of this form of diet in which zero animal things are allowed, such as milk. Veggie fans, then again, cut meat out however frequently cheerfully consume milk-based objects, very similar to cheddar, and possibly even devour a regular helping of eggs.

Now you get the Regular"veggie enthusiast" who

believes restricted amounts of fish to a wonderful extent.

I know a woman that professes to be a vegan nonetheless eats bacon and fish (if this bodes well). There is a word for her book image of vegetarianism: Wikipedia characterizes her "semi-vegan."

The purpose, however, is that a Plant-based eating routine is to a degree vague in actual definition and spreads a broad range of different eating rehearses - you will find not any real hard fast rules aside from the overall incorporation of heaps of crops and evasion of beef.

No matter camp of vegetarianism that an Individual decides to pursue, nobody could deny that it requires the conduct of the mill person a particular level of self-restraint to carry this up in any of its structures. Not only on the grounds that it suggests no more fat, yummy steaks yet additionally as it takes is a challenging charge against what is anticipated in current day culture, and it leaves a critical burden when buying, eating out, or even eating at the dining table of a company.

So for why do Mr. Clinton And these other societal hotshots actually difficulty? Might it be worth the penances, and therefore are the healthcare benefits sufficiently unique to compensate for the most life makeover it asks?

We ought to take a peek.

What Is So Great About "Eatin' Your Veggies?"

The plant-based abstaining from excessive food intake routine as it is now coming from a growing pool of experts viewing something inalienably amiss with the Western eating pattern.

Fantastic many assessments found a plague-like scourge of continuous diseases in the western world also requires attention to the way the ascent of those ailments nonsensically in comparison with mechanical headway (particularly in horticulture).

Others call to focus on how regions of the presence at which the Western eating regime has not yet gotten, an eating pattern to a fantastic extent connected with financial advancement, do not endure the equal disturbing paces of those maladies. Truth be told, these sicknesses (which include corpulence, coronary disease, diabetes, and several kinds of cancerous expansion) are often alluded to in well-known articles as "Western disorders."

T. Colin Campbell, co-writer of all The momentous (and a few of those time questionable) novels concerning the matter, "The China Study: Startling Implications for Diet, Weight Loss, and Long-Term Health," ventures to ensure that "malignancy is a topographically limited illness." He maintains up that in the event you take a gander in an entire manual, the lands of the planet having the most notable disease rates clearly associate with all the zones of this presence where protein is a huge part of the diet.

Meat-based weight control programs, His camp acknowledges, would be the reprobate.

A multi-year veteran in Sustenance inquires, Dr. Campbell maintains a person eating regimen made from over 10 percent meat prompts a huge ascent in illness hazard... that's all. He compels, nevertheless a plant established eating routine even gets the capability to fix a body as a very long time past battered by degenerative disease and reestablish great health.

And bear in mind that Campbell Is definitely the most energetic, outspoken, and persuasive of this plant-based eating regime swarm, he is absolutely not alone.

Another evaluation as of late Dispersed at the Journal of the American Medical Association subtleties how Canadian scientists nourished issues with higher LDL cholesterol levels (which is the awful stuff) an eating regime portrayed by plant-based sterols, soy protein, soy milk, soy-based meat replacements, nuts, and oats.

At the Assortment of a half a year, the Subjects saw their LDL levels fall by a standard of 13 percent - corrosion that likens to an 11% fall in the threat of a stroke in the subsequent decade.

Another guardian of the eating regular, Caldwell B. Esselstyn, MD, failed a multi-year probe plagued coronary disease patients that had the choice to stop their condition by intensifying in addition to completely reverse around it in 70 percent of cases.

Additionally, What About Weight Loss?

Extraordinary inquiry.

Another extraordinary Benefit Of those plant-driven eating regimens is they will generally lead to crucial, exceptionally reliable weight loss. Among the principal reasons for this good symptom is that red meats and especially singed nourishments are far more calorically thick compared to are water-based staples such as the regular products of their soil.

Supplant a larger piece of nourishment in your plate together with the crops, and the last product is that you consume fewer calories and you also get in shape faster. Simple, really.

Truth be told, one investigation explicitly identified with weight-loss checked African American women, a statistic particularly inclined to corpulence, contrasting areas who ate a normally plant-based eating routine with those generally devouring seared nourishments and red meat. They discovered the following gathering placed on more weight within the multiyear research.

The analysts hurried to bring up The way both parties would generally eat a similar amount of nutrition, however the calories were much higher for the following gathering. This manner, it had been the high-caloric depth of beef and seared nourishment that resulted in the massive weight gains.

Can you see where this is about?

Outfitting Your Internal Herbivore

If that the Plant-based eating regimen seems great to you nevertheless you do not know if you are educated enough to go "quickly" on beef, a fundamental hint for exchanging on your eating regime without making it too difficult on your own would be to start slowly, with continuous alterations.

Have a stab at ridding out a few suppers seven times with veggie enthusiast nutrition choices. Or on the flip side supplant a few issue things that you use a fantastic deal with more valuable different possibilities, separately - there are actually some really tasty and persuading meat choices out there today, as an example. Another chance is to decide on a few times seven days to "give it a chance" being a veggie fan.

On the long haul, these Straightforward decisions can become a typical bit of your brand new, more favorable eating regimen, and you're going to pick up the drive for extreme alterations.

Work a few veggies, similar to Beans, to your eating regimen too. They are high in protein and fiber, plus they supplant some of the calories you are missing - some weight watchers find slack in energy levels when shifting to a plant-overwhelmed diet without including a considerable substitution.

At last, recall concerning the individual tendency to consume similar sections no matter what stays on our plate. Stunt yourself by putting more space in your plate with goods of the ground, leaving space for the toxic stuff.

For intense health, 80 percent of your eating regimen

should be made from "water-based" nourishments - I suggest foods increased from the floor.

Try it and comprehend the best way to feel.

A Word On Keeping It Simple

To the extent just how rough your Plant-based eating routine should be, it is really a thing of which of those processes of reasoning you pursue and the way bad-to-the-bone you're about near home nourishment concept.

Is all-out veganism the primary genuine vegetarian eating pattern? Are veggie fans who consume a tiny fish and perhaps the occasional reddish meat dish (wheeze) going to vegan damnation?

It is an individual choice, however here is my take you won't find numerous eating regimens out there which do not concede grubbing back on an increased volume of these old fashioned new products of the ground and reducing the red meat whilst bringing your calories down won't perform ponders to your health, your looks, and your waist.

Know about these benefits and Listen to them really.

But before you get excessively intense with your new diet program, realize that a successful eating regimen is a balance between near home requirements, personal gratification, and health. Additional it's completely possible to take a transcendently plant-based eating regimen without giving up your soul to the veggie garden and completely prohibiting cheeseburgers to get a remarkable rest.

A nice diet plan is kept up through essential principles, and also a rare cheat now and again (if you've got it leveled out) does not make you an awful person or imply you are a double-crosser of an unclear, vague family. When you have put up powerful dietary routines, cheating may even be something worth being grateful for sometimes.

Certainly, there is a great deal of study on the market bringing up some intriguing issues regarding meat and the possible damage it can do to our own bodies (especially in large quantities), yet more research is as required prior to any absolutes are solved. In the meantime, just utilize some fantastic judgment.

Michael Pollan probably puts it Greatest in his novel, "In Defense of Food," if he outlines his own recommendations for plant-eating everything considered: "Eat nutrition. Not really that much. Generally plants"

It does not' get any complex than this, and any person out there expecting to secure the health and weight reduction benefits of a reasonable wholesome eating regimen without placing themselves through primitive broccoli training camp could be wise to pursue his simple method of thinking.

Outfitting yourself with advice, in view of the fact, about sustenance, consuming fewer calories and exercise is essential about the off possibility that you're not thinking about becoming more healthy, keeping it off and carrying on having a more favorable means of life.

Why A Plant-Based Diet Matters

There is not a lot of riddles about a 'wholesome eating pattern' however it may be fascinating to consider to get a bit on the incomprehensibility of what it holds for you.

Entire Foods

Right off the bat, a plant-based eating routine perceives the opinion of ordinary, whole nourishments, not calories or supplements, as the crucial unit of sustenance. This is due to the synergistic mixture of minerals, nutrients, cancer prevention representatives and phytochemicals that could just happen with whole nourishments. Hence it bodes well to possess moderate steps of various whole nourishments on your eating regimen regularly.

This nonstop exchanging around one form of vegetable, whole grain or organic merchandise for a different until you have all of the many sorts of phytochemicals well within your own body is important for intense health. Additionally, various portions of the body need identifying plant artificial concoctions to operate; along those lines, a solid blend of nutritional supplements is essential to good health.

Colors of Organic Foods

Further, a vegetarian ingesting Routine is similarly about eating the colors. Combining a variety of colors and types of foods grown on the floor is equally solid and inviting. Truth be told, colors provide signals to the nutritional supplements they feature.

For example, red shows Nutrient A (beta carotene) and nutritional supplement C. Firmly after, it is yellowish, which is a sign of fiber and potassium; whereas green methods it's pressed iron or folic corrosive. Further, purple and blue colors reveal the nearness of anthocyanins that combat free radicals; along with white sparkles with minerals and nutrients.

Mending Power of Foods

Eminently, the recovering Intensity of complete nourishments within a plant-based eating regimen is available for you in the event you would like to use it.

Be as it may, this type of fixing is solely from time to time fast; Nature has to be allowed to follow all of the ways through and there aren't any health supernatural occurrences medium-term.

In the meantime, the ready nourishments on your eating regimen can offset all of the fantastic work of food resources in a matter of minutes. Everything you do and do not eat is tremendously important in the event you would like to see positive results.

Green Blood of Plants

As it had been, a plant-based eating Regular is allowing in sunlight on your life if you consume lush greens using a high degree of chlorophyll. In fact, your own red blood flowers with all the green blood of crops. This manner, the further greens you've got within the own body, the greater oxygen to supply crimson platelets for you. Likewise as the trees depend upon the leaves for nutrition, it is possible to endure presence with lush greens.

Nourishment Planning

In the end, a vegetarian ingesting regime believes about the way nourishments are eaten or arranged; so you need to gain from fresh nourishments or crisply prepared nutrition. There was a situation where re-warmed stays were served to some woman in repression. From this point onwards, her health went down and she dropped all her energy, not having the choice to hold down any daily job.

The Foundation of Good Health for Trainers

The benefits of wholesome Improvements have been paraded right, left and concentrate from the health field now. What many common Americans fail to listen to is that for its improvements to generate full effects, an individual ought to make nutrition-based sustenance the basis of the health. Preferably, the improvements should only be used to expand the hard to acquire nutritional supplements.

The ideal nutrition counselor that people can get would be to assemble their eating regimens connected to plant things. This suggests one wants to consume more natural goods, whole vegetables and grains. Fats are also a substantial bit of solid sustenance, yet should be based on strong polyunsaturated fats as it had been. Canola and olive oils drop from a good course. Another substantial trick to healthful nourishment based sustenance is that the requirement to maintain the calories in audio extents. Expending a larger quantity of calories than the body can use as a guideline prompts weight reduction.

Perfect wellbeing through nourishment can be achieved if folks work out how to consume fantastic starches in complete grains. Instead of what people think, starches aren't bad for the entire body. Or perhaps, it's tasteful and preparing they encounter prior to being placed on the shop's retires which make them demolishes the many fantastic elements inside them.

An individual should similarly concentrate on protein resources he consolidates from the eating regime. The very best protein wellsprings of carbohydrates include legumes, fish, poultry, nuts and dried poultry. More importantly, the eating regime should possess sufficient fiber. Fiber is available from whole grains, products of the ground. More importantly, an individual ought to join a variety of organic products in their own eating regimen. Nutritionists accept that delightfully shaded products of this soil have more minerals and nutrients.

In that capacity, an individual should opt for the dark orange, red, green and yellow veggies and organic products. Broadly, a strong eating regimen should include nutrients, organic goods, fats, vegetables, proteins, fiber and sugars. An individual needs to perhaps consider dietary improvements in the event he is not getting sufficient natural or mineral products.

The best beginning place to strong nourishment based sustenance is just one's kitchen. By stocking the kitchen with strong nourishments, the likelihood of eating and preparing unlucky suppers is extremely diminished. If you're searching for nourishment items, an individual should integrate crisp veggies and organic products because of their top-most need. Carrots, spinach, apples, onions and garlic ought to make this rundown for any client. If you're searching for grain, then substitute white grains for whole grains. Consider purchasing dark colored rice, bulgur, and grain. Quinoa and oat berries are other sound options.

If you are looking for proteins, dodge the compulsion to purchase a source of red meat to keep on your fridge. Or perhaps, select more valuable alternatives of poultry, fish, legumes, eggs, nuts and lentils. Red meat should be consumed once in a while however less a part of the day daily diet. Instead of carbohydrates, an individual ought to select oils to get pan-searing, overall cooking and garnish sandwiches.

Directions to Attain Great Nutrition by Eating a Plant-Based Diet

Vegetarianism and veganism are ways of life that are characterized by the utilization of animal items from garments and nourishment, and limiting animal testing and remorselessness. In vegetarianism and veganism, the eating regime is plant-based and averts meat. Even though it may seem to be missing to prevent meat at the eating regimen, a plant established eating regimen really can give all of the essential supplements a body should maintain good wellbeing and progress life.

A plant established eating routine comprises an organic solvent, veggies, nuts, and seeds. Each of them contains all of the supplements the body should advance good absorption, mobile capability and repair, heart health, bone health, as well as emotional health. Simultaneously, they're low in fat, calories, and cholesterol. They assist to keep up weight whilst providing satisfactory steps of fiber, sugars, nutrients, and mobile reinforcements.

The best strategy to ensure there's a sufficient stockpile of this substantial variety of nutritional supplements anticipated to have a good mien would be to change the plant up established nourishments that are consumed. You will find a few to navigate so the possible outcomes for variety are superior to whatever one would expect. The ingestion regimen comprises servings of greens and fresh all-natural solution, yet additionally comprises grain products, legumes, oils, herbs, and tastes. All together, these items can be combined and coordinated and organized in various ways to acquire the steps of nutritional supplements necessary for great health, without making improvements.

Plant-based nourishments include Amino acids, different nutrients, fiber, protein and magnesium, an entirely indispensable supplement for great health, amongst others. They are sometimes discovered in a couple of nourishments. A couple of nourishments have a fantastic deal of particular nutritional supplements and only a bit of the other, that's why assortment is firmly prescribed for a plant established eating regimen. Here are a few supplements which need to be inadequate stock from nutrition, and it's vital to pay particular head to and try to expend them in every meal.

Calcium is one supplement the human body needs for strong bones and teeth, yet it is not made or place away within the body. To acquire a satisfactory loaf of salt, lush greens have to be a principle staple of a plant established eating regimen. These include kale, spinach, bok choy, collard, mustard and turnip greens. Almonds and hazelnuts could be inserted into a feast to get a few extra calcium.

Iron is important from the automobile of oxygen to the organs within the body. Verdant greens really are a good wellspring of iron, nevertheless distinct things will provide the basic iron too. In order to expend sufficient iron onto a plant established eating regimen, nourishments such as cereal, whole wheat pieces of bread, and lentils, along with a couple of different food resources. Iron-rich nourishments should be devoured all of the time.

Nutrient B12 is one nutrient we need, yet is not bottomless in plant established weight control programs. B12 is seen in continual nourishments and improvements. This simple nutrient has an effect in providing us energy, reduces the threat of a couple of ailments, and aids with generally talking psychological well-being, therefore it ought to be an ordinary bit of the plant established eating routine.

The nourishments of this ground in Their common arrangement are unaltered and in this way more beneficial for individuals than animal cooked and based nourishments. With a bit of research and also the use of the variety, a person could efficiently achieve incredible wellbeing and also an all-around adjusted method of life by adopting a plant established eating regimen.

Observing A Plant-Based Diet Can Be Easy With Home Gardens

Various individuals today are visiting a plant-based eating regime instead compared to abstains from food too rich in saturated meat products, shoddy nutrition, and profoundly managed food resources. Occasionally, it involves investing more energy at the manufacturing segment of your local grocery store, hunting for leafy foods that are manufactured naturally and spending extra cash on these.

You can chase an outstanding Plant-based eating routine in a way and away superior manner whilst developing your meals grown from the floor on your home nursery. In case you reside in a condominium, you may start a holder backyard prior to a glowing window. In case you've got a plot of land to change into a nursery you are able to pull all the stops with a nursery filled up with strong foods grown on the floor. You're able to develop nearly anything at a tiny nursery so you've got the spring, summer and fall to consume off your own territory.

Vegetables Readily Grown At Home

Tomatoes loan themselves nicely to holder planting and may develop like crazy in the fantastic ground of your backyard. The age and develop during the whole year so that you can select what you need for sandwiches, portions of mixed greens, snacks, fresh sauces and in any case, for grinding.

You can create your own peas Or legumes in a bowl or on your patio garden. They're full of phytonutrients that have their extreme intensity on the off possibility that you essentially pick exactly what you need and consume them at the first opportunity; you've got the ideal measure of strong phytonutrients and cancer prevention brokers in the nutrition not long after choosing them.

Peppers, zucchini, carrots, broccoli, and greens such as Kale are exceptional choices for a house garden and allow you to go after strong and excessively new create throughout the whole summer and into the autumn.

Your Home Garden

In the event that you choose to have a backyard house nursery, you need to pick in the event you want to come up with organic nourishments or never. Organic planting is the most perfect choice in light of how nutrition is manufactured with additives, herbicides, or fungicides. This means no hurtful synthetic chemicals exist together with the nutrition you select and you may also eat them straight from their nursery without washing them extensively.

Grow a Wide Selection of Nourishments that become prepared at different occasions of this interval:

Radishes, for example, take only half a month to acquire palatably and, following to yanking them up, you've got space to cultivate a pillar of something distinct. The huge bulk develops tomatoes and a couple of men and women develop lettuce, carrots, and potatoes.

The 2 potatoes and squash need the entire summer to receive available for eating so that you need to just to keep them weed and watch them grow. From the first autumn or pre-fall, you can find the sausage and collect the skillet. These types of products can be held at room temperature or in a cool place for quite a while so that you have instant winter eating from veggies you designed in the spring.

Lettuce and distinct greens can be developed and gathered throughout the whole summer for the very best in dishes of mixed greens that are full of phytonutrients and mobile reinforcements. You ought to simply collect some of the leaves, wash them and enjoy them in a solid serving of mixed greens with carrots, tomatoes, or radishes you developed yourself. This is the middle of a plant-based eating regimen which will provide you advantages away beyond a meat-based eating regimen.

Meat-based ingestion regimens are low in cancer prevention representatives and saturated in saturated fats. It's possible to find the sustenance you want from organic and vegetables products that you develop yourself to be a known reduction in fatty shops in your classes and a lesser chance for coronary disease and stroke. There's a diminished threat of particular tumors using very low fat, plant-based eating routine.

Show signs of advancement Outcomes With Composting

On the off Possibility that you want an especially productive nursery, consider starting a mulch pile or box. You ought to simply place in plant and clippings from around your lawn, include nourishment pieces and paper, mixing everything with a bit of dirt. Worms flourish from the moist condition of a nice fertilizer load together with the aim you will before long have these items changed into rich soil which will make your normal nursery flourish.

Begin Today

You will find a Lot of aides Online for organic vegetable planting, and many books on the subject. As a rule of thumb, the ideal teacher is comprehension, so obtain proficiency with the inherent progress, get the terms and manage a business! Be certain that you find the kids linked to the nursery also; it's an outstanding learning experience, and also an unbelievable opportunity to get to know one another.

CHAPTER TWO

YOUR PLANT-BASED KITCHEN

I left a rundown for you to use when it is time to market your kitchen and clean area. It is a comprehensive rundown yet do not hesitate. It is only a guideline to supply you with an idea of this range of nourishments overall nutrition plant-based eating regime.

Start with what you as of today have on your kitchen and clean area. If that you are feeling overpowered, begin with a few different vegetables, grains, herbs and flavors, dried organic goods, seeds and nuts, berries and routine meals are grown on the floor. After a time, add new items to your menu. Provided that you will have accumulated the larger part of these things beneath or may have at any speed tried all of them.

Rundown of nourishments to inventory at home

Whole grains, pasta and breakfast oats

Rice (darker, black, reddish), quinoa, Grain, antiquated wheat assortments spelled and farro, whole wheat, buckwheat, oats, millet, sorghum (without gluten), rye and triticale (cross strain of wheat and rye), and things made of these whole grains (pasta, lasagne, noodles, oats, flours, breads).

Vegetables

Lentils (red, dark-colored, Green, dim), beans (pinto, white, crimson, dark, kidney, dark peered toward, etc.), chickpeas. Store them afterward cook yourself or get them in containers and jars. There is also pasta made from lentil flour.

Herbs and tastes, dried

This rundown could be exceptionally Long, especially in the event you enjoy Indian nutrition, yet coming next is a vital inventory to start: sea salt, pepper (dark, reddish, white, green), bean stew bits, paprika powder, and curry powder or paste, garlic, garlic powder, and onion drops, solid leaves, lavender, lavender, lavender, basil, educated, organic vegetable soup powder, caraway seeds, mustard seeds, cinnamon, cardamom, nutmeg, ginger powder.

Herbs and tastes, fresh

Basil, parsley, coriander, Rosemary, rosemary, chamomile, ginger.

Dried natural products

Prunes, dates, figs, raisins, apricots, goji berries, mulberries.

Crisp (according to season) or solidified berries

Blueberries, dark currants, red Currantsfruits, raspberries, strawberries, blackberries.

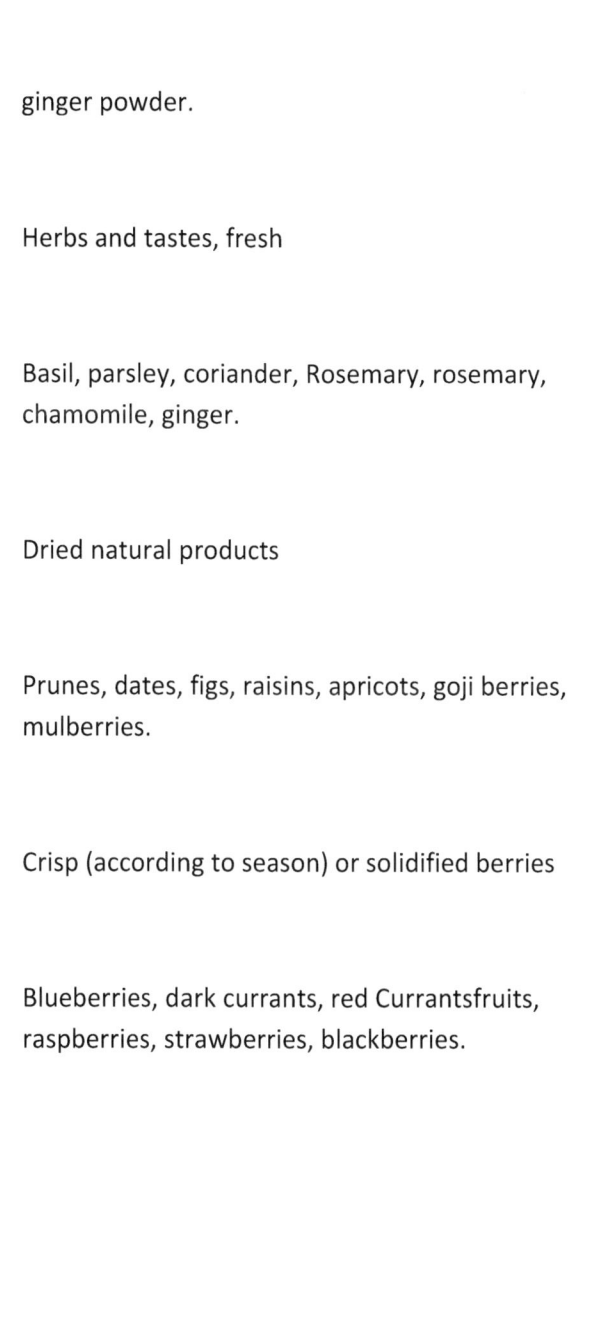

Nuts and seeds

Flax seeds, chia seeds, hemp seeds, sesame seeds, sunflower seeds, pumpkin seeds, poppy seeds, Brazil nuts, pecans, cashews, hazelnuts, almonds, crushed coconut.

Notice: ideally eat seeds, nuts, vegetables and grains which were splashed and washed. Drenching creates them more efficiently edible, reduces or expels phytic corrosive (which reduces nutrient ingestion); releases the protein inhibitors which keep nutritional supplements while growing and expects untimely germination, and also raise nutrient B material.

Verdant plates and greens of Mixed greens

Romaine lettuce, ice sheet lettuce, arugula, chard, kale, spinach, bok choy, watercress, radicchio, endive, chicory.

Ocean expansion

Wakame, kombu, nori, agar-agar.

Boring vegetables

Potatoes, sweet potatoes, Parsnips, corn, pumpkin, butternut squash, pine seed skillet, green beans, plantains.

Non-boring veggies

Artichokes, beetroot, turnip, carrots, summer squash, chime peppers, tomatoes, leeks, onions, eggplant, cucumber, celery, broccoli, cauliflower, cabbage (green, red, Savoy, Chinese), Brussels develops, green beans, asparagus, okra, radishes, sugar snap peas, mushrooms.

Natural products

Bananas, apples, apples, pears, mandarins, avocados, lemons, kiwis, olives, persimmons, mangos, grapefruit, watermelon, melon.

Additional

Cosmetic yeast, cacao powder, carob powder, dim chocolate (if 72% cacao material) or cacao paste, cider vinegar.

Useful for people on the transfer and For rare treats

Soy sauce (look for one which Includes a very low sodium content), agave syrup, xylitol, stevia.

Eateries and bistros are adequate options when fulfilling companions or about the off possibility which you will need to have a rest in the kitchen. I am aware that it's tough to find places that take into consideration plant-based entire nourishments however it is inclined to be completed.

When Exercising, settle veggie enthusiast or vegan cafés or eateries offering a few veggie enthusiast items in their own menus. Do your examination using Happy Cow (happycow.net).

Assess the internet menus of fresh places. If you don't understand any incontrovertible options for you, at the point phone or email the base and ask as to if it is going to oblige you.

As of now in a café? Ask as To if they own a veggie fan menu.

Make Sure You indicate you would like a Dinner free of monster items. Regularly folks do not have the foggiest notion what veggie enthusiast or plant-based approaches and you'll probably end up using milk or cheddar in your plate.

Try to not be timid about creating Your own dish out of the ingredients from the menu. Many eateries should be pleased to support you.

Eat until you consume it. Once in the Café, you'll be able to organize a serving of greens or even a bowl of vegetable soup. Every eatery should, at any rate, have one of these 2 things.

Cultural cafés are in each situation Fantastic options for finding veggie enthusiasts or vegetarian dinners. You can at any speed get vegetables and rice. Create a point to ask the culinary pros forget about all of the oil and salt, on the off possibility they can.

Serving of mixed greens Smorgasbords can be ample. Keep this simple plate guideline: 1/2 non-bland veggies (primitive and cooked), 1/4 whole grains and dull veggies and 1/4 protein (seeds, nuts, vegetables).

On the off possibility that there's No whole nourishment dressing in the plate of mixed greens pub, use vegetable noodle soup, veggie curry or merely lemon peel. This is going to support you with starting to admit slimmer alternatives too.

A Couple of eateries Provide macrobiotic Options, for example a dish cooked with no salt and oils, simply lean and straightforward whole nourishments. I've had the choice to discover a couple of lunch areas in this way in Barcelona.

If you Realize the protein some section of the feast will be more pliable, solicit them to substitute a few from the protein together with veggies, whole grains, nuts/seeds or avocados.

Pastries look yummy at cafés However it is generally better to skirt the desserts. They're commonly high fat and fatty vessels. There are specific cases and a couple of spots provide primitive candies such as chia-pudding or nutty snacks without added sugar and oils.

Constantly be affable and cordial towards café staff and your sidekicks. In the event you're fine to them, everything considered, they will be acceptable for you. Constantly be appreciative after that the team has qualified your requirements.

The above being said, do roster Outside an improvement. I generally urge people to ask without petroleum, plant-based and whole grain choices no matter if I recognize that the place does not offer them. On the off chance that people continue asking these determinations, at the point who understands? 1 day the eatery can add them to the menu.

OK Purchase a Juicer or even a Blender on a Plant-Based Diet?

Investigating a juicer that the primary Thing that appeared and caught my attention was clearly the price. They aren't modest. Whatever the situation, buying a fire pit to cook steaks on is not a fryer to get fricasseeing, therefore I put this to the side. The cost actually does not create a difference in the event you're doing so to your wellbeing. Only saying.

Favorable situation

I discovered that squeezing isolates The juice out of the mash. It believes a far dissolvable fiber that keeps water on your digestive organs. That supports noise microscopic organisms on your gut. Squeezing is an unbelievable option with respect to detoxing you are frame. If that becoming more healthy is 1 thing you are trying to reach, at the point I definitely would buy a juicer. It's by far the most well-known choice when folks are considering this type of progress.

Disservices

At the stage Once I was shooting a Gander in the hindrances, I really merely found a couple of things others referenced while performing research. They're pricey and also a whole lot more difficult to wash. That's it, everybody seems to cherish their juicers.

Mixing Advantages And Disadvantages

Favorable Conditions

That is my top Option Because I enjoy the way I get everything out of the products of the ground. It disturbs nothing. For me, that suggests it's considerably more insoluble fiber. In 50 years old it tops off me and keeps me considerably more habitual in my gut along with a superior stool. Mixing causes me to reinforce my burden when getting each of the supplements in the previous product. Furthermore, my favorite bit of leeway is that they are able to add super nourishments into the blender.

- Blueberries

- Acai Berries

- Goji Berries

- Cacao In the event you're mixing a shack with almond milk.

- Chia seeds

- Hemp seeds

That's simply naming a few, You get my point. Since you're drinking a larger sum of the mash it allows you are body to keep the sugars much slower digesting my glucose file. I feel unbelievable with any lengthier energy levels. That's only me you should choose yourself. A blender is also much less expensive and that I think I use it for various functions also. It's a whole lot easier to wash also.

Drawbacks

Well I'd really like a Complaint about this if some of you have some musings on hindrances. In all actuality, it's my favorite alternative and completely love blending. Tell me you are concerned about the comments area underneath.

Should not something be said about Advantages OF BOTH

This is my contemplations on This, how could it be dreadful to put more meals grown in the earth into you are diet daily? Both these options give excellent benefits with fiber on your gut-related course. The healthcare benefits alone should be sufficient for anyone to should create the subsequent stride and comprise either the batter or blender into your own kitchen arms stockpile.

I have a past full of medical Issues in my loved ones, generally cardiovascular disease. Just by doing the two of These choices you can definitely diminish you are chance of a stroke by 26%. Currently, I'm not a professional and I've just discovered this information While performing the mining myself on the health facet of it. Likewise, Alzheimer's illness is something I have my own contemplations on also. Been stated by adding vegetables might help prevent or delay the motion On this particular infection. That is another reason I transferred to some plant-based eating regimen. I believe that with the growth hormones contributed to the animals we Expend, it is the most important supply too. Too the synthetics we place on the No-natural create. That is just another article for another time.

Choosing

I will say this however, I carry on with a plant-based way of life and have made changes, this is only one of them. As I would see it is totally up to you which course you might want to go to. Regardless of whether you mix or squeeze you are rolling out the improvement for your wellbeing. I have shed more than 80 pounds and diminished my circulatory strain down to typical, all by practice and changing my way of life. In the event that creation changes whichever way makes you feel good and live more, wouldn't you do it in any case? In case you're hoping to purchase possibly one pick the one that you will keep on utilizing each day for your family's wellbeing.

Recall that in case you're joining diverse organic product juices to either mix, you could be affecting the last item. On the off chance that the sugar levels are high in the juices, at that point you're somewhat invalidating the point. Indeed, even the solidified natural product has a wide range of added substances and sugar. Make sure to peruse every one of the marks before you mix everything together. Likewise, one mix-up numerous individuals make is adding too many natural products to their juicer or blender. In case you're attempting to get thinner it may in reality moderate weight lose down. I like to mix straight vegetables and from time to time I will include some sort of organic product. Recall that I referenced the super nourishments? I really add a greater amount of those to make the most sound shake.

In the event that I don't want to haul out the nourishment processor, I will utilize my blender to mix elements for my veggie-lover burgers and hummus. So there are different things that you can utilize a blender for.

Natural Herbal Plants For Better Health

Customers are getting progressively mindful of the conditions that their nourishment is developed under, which has prompted a flood in enthusiasm for natural homegrown cultivating. In addition, there is presently developing attention to the wellbeing and therapeutic cures conceivable with natural homegrown planting.

Natural prescription and natural homegrown planting are not finished substitutes for current drugs, and there are numerous situations where you will be better off with mechanically incorporated meds. In any case, there is an extraordinary number of normal afflictions that can be relieved and even avoided through less unforgiving plant-based plans.

The perspective of homegrown medication is one of thinking about the entire life-form and not simply the indications. Thus two individuals who visit a professional and have comparative side effects might be proposed to take very various cures.

Individuals who go to natural homegrown cultivating to develop regular drugs are generally exceptionally mindful of their bodies and furthermore of their environment, and spot a great deal of significance on the quality and provenance of the nourishment that they expend.

Regardless of whether you are an accomplished natural planter or simply beginning with regular therapeutic herbs, you will likely share the desire to control the root of groceries and other substantial admissions with individuals with a similar intrigue.

Truth be told natural cultivating is experiencing a renaissance, yet very few individuals are yet mindful that similar rules that can be applied to natural nourishment are likewise substantial for plant-based prescriptions. What's more, less yet realize that it is so natural to develop homegrown cures at home!

There are a few different ways to devour naturally developed restorative plants. The most effortless one is just to eat them, regardless of whether crude or cooked, and numerous remedial plants are a piece of typical kitchen utilization, for example, garlic or pepper.

With respect to the approaches to expend meds originating from natural homegrown cultivating, there are numerous healing plants that can be essentially eaten. Many, for example, ginger root, are basic in the kitchen, yet doses and admission normally vary.

You can likewise plan natural teas and mixes. Also, ingesting natural herbs isn't the best way to expend them. You can likewise get ready emollients and creams with numerous naturally planted herbs, and use them to ease hurts and irritations.

The Convenience of Having a Kitchen Garden in Your Backyard

Developed right outside of the home, the accommodation of having a kitchen garden in your lawn can be very efficient. In this day and age of huge general stores, most don't have kitchen plants any longer and a wide range of nourishments are accessible all year with no immediate exertion of having developed them. Regardless of this appeal, the comfort of having a kitchen garden is still genuine, and until you've attempted the heavenliness of homegrown oregano in your pasta sauce that was picked directly outside your secondary passage, you may not understand what you are absent.

There are some underlying work and venture engaged with any nursery, however, be amazingly straightforward and not a great deal of work or speculation. You can put resources into structuring a little region and have it finished to make a wonderful lawn nursery, or you can buy a couple of huge pots and have them fixed outside of your secondary passage for simple access. What's progressively significant about your kitchen garden is the thing that you decide to develop.

Numerous individuals with kitchen gardens decide to develop herb plants that they would routinely buy at the supermarket. This is particularly mainstream with settlers from different nations. They regularly bring or request seeds from their local countries and develop them on here in their kitchen cultivates with the goal that they can keep on getting a charge out of a considerable lot of similar nourishments that they depended upon in their nations of origin. For instance, Italian migrants used to have gardens loaded up with flavors and greens that they utilized in Italy in their ordinary cooking and to help supplement what they bought here. Asians brought over seeds of harsh melon and different cabbages for staples in their cooking. Numerous half and half dishes have been made that way and are staples in American cooking today.

Beginning with enduring herbs and lasting vegetables that are extraordinarily simple to develop crops is prescribed. Rosemary, chives, oregano, thyme, sage, rhubarb, and asparagus make a decent base for including yearly herbs and vegetables. These base herbs will convey any cook all through numerous dishes summer through winter. Enhanced yearly herbs can be collected and solidified or got for dry season use.

Regular vegetables that are famous for kitchen gardens are tomatoes. As the nations' most famous nursery vegetable, the tomato makes the foundation of most kitchen gardens and for an incredible explanation. Prepared right off of the vine in the late spring, tomatoes are a genuine treat straight from the back yard! They taste a lot better and adjusted than market tomatoes, and with the treasure restoration tomatoes are likewise excellent and differed fit as a fiddle and surfaces.

Peppers are another lawn garden top choice. They also can be effectively protected and delighted in crisp, and developing your very own peppers will set aside your bunches of cash on shopping for food. In the event that you've never delighted in the medical advantages and simplicity of developing delectable crisp peppers before you should. Indeed, even kitchen cultivates in the far north can appreciate a gather of sweet peppers with the correct assortments developed. The two tomatoes and peppers areas effectively developed in compartments as they are in the ground.

Lettuces and different greens are another extraordinary

regular kitchen garden increases. There are numerous sorts of lettuce with numerous flavors, a considerable lot of which you can regularly just discover in extravagant costly eateries. Develop them yourself at home and appreciate gourmet directly outside of your indirect access inexpensively! Other occasional greens, for example, swiss chard, solid spinach, cabbage, and microgreens are on the whole costly from the store as well and are so natural to develop at home. Get a good deal on shopping for food by developing your very own greens.

Today, families are eating more beneficial and are progressively worried about the quality and taste of their nourishment. In case you're as yet not secure with the comfort of a kitchen garden, have a go at growing a couple of plants in holders and watch your family appreciate the simplicity of picking new herbs for adding to the family supper. Kids love developing and gathering these nourishments and the kitchen nursery can turn into a task for the whole family!

The most effective method to Create a Plant-Based Kitchen You Love

What is your preferred room in the house? Mine is the

kitchen. You may believe that is clear however it wasn't constantly similar to that. Before I became vegetarian, I once in a while cooked. My kitchen was modest yet it was still more space than I required; the cabinet that held my take-out menus was excessively little, notwithstanding. My companions prodded me that I claimed one pot and I never at any point utilized it. When I became a veggie-lover, be that as it may, everything changed. There was no place to eat in my neighborhood so I needed to figure out how to cook. The more I cooked, the more the kitchen turned into the most significant room. It was the place I made plans and cooked for those I adored. I understood that realizing how to cook was just a piece of the procedure. The kitchen itself caused cooking to appear to be more enthusiastically or simpler, contingent upon the condition of the room. On the off chance that cooking appears an excess of work or baffling, it doesn't need to mean you loathe cooking. It may be that your kitchen needs a makeover into space where motivation streams and inventiveness flourishes. The kitchen is the core of the home so put your heart into your kitchen. Here are a few hints to make a plant-based kitchen you love.

1. Put things in place

the kitchen will be a room you invest a great deal of

energy in, it ought to be satisfying to your eye and make you feel good and cheerful. Paint your kitchen with an upbeat shading. Enhance the dividers with prints, photographs and motivational plaques. Get fun magnets to hang pictures, plans or your kids' work of art on the cooler. Purchase a non-slip tangle to pad your feet at the sink. Inspire your plant-based eating by keeping a bowl of the brilliant organic product on your counter. Consider an indoor herb garden on your window ledge for the smell and having new herbs readily available. Keep an iPod dock or radio so you can chime in while hacking veggies. A need for me is a book that remains to hold a cookbook open to a most loved formula. Have a couple of red accents in the room – red animates the craving! Obviously, it's up to the kind of stylistic theme you like yet basically when a room is pretty and feels inviting, you will need to invest more energy in it.

2. Allow it to stream

You might not have a ton of state about the design of your kitchen particularly things like where the stove and fridge are or how much counter space you have. In any case, you can take advantage of what you need to make a workspace that is productive and utilitarian. On the off chance that you don't have a lot of cupboards for pots and dish, consider hanging a pot rack. Contingent upon the room, it tends to be in the kitchen over the island or against a divider. In my first modest kitchen, my better half balanced a bar in the little open entryway of the kitchen and I hung my pots and skillet from snares. It was space-sparing as well as it made a truly cool gateway. In the event that you don't have a ton of counter space, purchase a major cutting board and spot it over the sink while cooking. Attempt to have your cutting board close to the stove so you can hack and drop. Keep the cooking utensils, oils, vinegar and different things you utilize most close to your work zone or stove for simple reach. Drape your flavors on the divider or get attractive zest holders to hold tight the ice chest. It's simpler to cook while all that you need is close by.

3. Be Organized

Cooking is significantly increasingly fun when you don't sit around looking for fixing or utensils. Arrange your storeroom things in gatherings. Keep every one of your flavors in a single spot, every one of your grains and beans in another, and every one of your containers, jars and jugs in another. Get clear containers for your grains, beans and vegetables and print names on them. I like to keep all my heating supplies like flours, preparing powder and sugars assembled. Have all your heating dishes in one spot. On the off chance that you don't have bureau space, get a bin to hold them. Keep your veggie lover cookbooks on a rack in the kitchen for motivation and snappy reference. Additionally hold a note pad to write down your very own thoughts for plans or your shopping list.

4. The Food

When you have your kitchen set up the manner in which you need it, it's a great opportunity to fill the storeroom and ice chest with all that you have to make astonishing plant-based dishes.

5. Instruments of the Trade

One of the principal things I did when I became vegetarian was purchase another cutting board and another arrangement of pots and dishes. I needed to cook with devices that had never contacted creature items. You will need to have a Dutch Oven pot for stews and bean stews, an enormous pot to cook pasta in, a medium and little pan with covers for cooking grains, sauces and flavors, and 8-inch and 10-inch skillets for pan-sears, sautés and sautéing veggie burgers. You will need a couple of huge preparing sheets for simmering vegetables and a meat dish that can go in the broiler. Regardless of whether you don't prepare a lot, you will likely need a biscuit tin, an 8-inch square brownie skillet, a rectangular portion search for gold or veggie lover meat portion and two 9-inch round cake dish. The most significant devices in any kitchen are the blades. Put resources into a decent culinary expert's blade, a bread blade and a paring blade. Get a couple of vegetable peelers with different sharp edges that cut in various shapes, a grater and a zester. With these fundamental instruments, you will have the option to make a million mind-blowing plant-based dishes.

6. Apparatuses and Gadgets

I'm very little of an apparatus and device individual. For me, the most significant apparatus is a nourishment processor as well as a fast blender. Contingent upon your financial limit, space, cooking needs and proclivity for machines, you may likewise need a submersion blender, a stand blender, a moderate cooker, a weight cooker, a rice cooker, and a waffle stove. Mainstream devices incorporate an electric can opener, a spiralizer for making veggie noodles, a pasta producer, hand blender, bread machines, juicers and frozen yogurt creators. It's a brilliant plan to just purchase what you truly require and have space for so you don't have a lot of devices occupying the room and gathering dust. I want to get things done by hand however that is my own inclination.

At the point when your kitchen is really, composed, productive, and well-supplied, it makes cooking to a greater extent a delight and to a lesser degree an errand. Rather than a room where work occurs, it turns into a sanctuary of imagination, motivation, and obviously, heavenliness. You may find that you can hardly wait to get into the kitchen and start making sound and delectable plant-based dishes.

CHAPTER THREE

4 WEAK MEAL PLAN

Veggie lover abstains from food have been connected to an assortment of medical advantages, including improved weight the board and assurance against certain constant illnesses.

In any case, finding adjusted, solid suppers on a

vegetarian diet can frequently be troublesome and overpowering.

On the off chance that inappropriately arranged, vegetarian diets may cause nourishing insufficiencies and medical issues.

The vegetarian diet is a type of dieting that kills every single creature item, including meat, fish, eggs, dairy, and nectar.

Individuals choose to receive veganism for various reasons, for example, moral concerns or strict standards.

Others may choose to become vegetarian to diminish their biological impression, as plant-based weight control plans are thought to produce less ozone harming substance discharges and utilize less characteristic assets.

All things considered, the natural effect of any eating regimen relies upon various variables, including how nourishments are created, bundled, and shipped.

Some additionally choose to pursue a veggie-lover diet for wellbeing reasons, as veganism is related to a huge number of advantages and may even help anticipate certain constant illnesses.

Specifically, vegetarian eats less have been appeared to improve heart wellbeing, increment weight reduction, and bolster glucose control.

Veggie lover shopping list

A sound veggie lover diet ought to contain an assortment of entire grains, proteins, solid fats, and leafy foods.

Nourishments like nuts, seeds, vegetables, soy items, and healthful yeast would all be able to help support your protein consumption for the duration of the day.

In the interim, avocado oil, coconut oil, and olive oil are

nutritious, vegetarian cordial decisions for sound fats.

Here is an example of a veggie lover shopping rundown to help kick you off.

Crisp produce

• Vegetables: asparagus, ringer peppers, broccoli, cabbage, carrots, cauliflower, garlic, kale, onions, potatoes, spinach, tomatoes, zucchini, and so on.

• Fruits: limes, pomegranates, apples, peaches, blueberries, grapes, grapefruit, lemons, kiwis, oranges, pears, strawberries,bananas, and so forth.

Solidified produce

• Vegetables: broccoli, Brussels grows, butternut squash, carrots, cauliflower, corn, green beans, peas, vegetable variety, and so on.

- Fruits: blackberries, blueberries, fruits, mangoes, pineapples, raspberries, strawberries, and so on.

Entire grains

- barley

- brown rice

- buckwheat

- bulgur

- farro

- oats

- quinoa

- sorghum

- teff

Bread and pasta

- brown rice pasta

- Whole-wheat pasta

- sprouted bread, for example, Ezekiel bread

- brown rice wraps

Protein sources

- Nuts: cashews, walnuts, almonds, Brazil nuts, hazelnuts, macadamia nuts, peanuts, pistachios, pecans, and so on.

- Seeds: pumpkin seeds, flax seeds, hemp seeds, sesame seeds, sunflower seeds, chia seeds, and so on.

- Legumes: lentils, chickpeas, kidney beans, naval force beans, pinto beans, dark beans, and so on.

- Soy items: tempeh, tofu, and so on.

- Protein powders: pea protein powder, dark-colored rice protein, hemp protein, and so on.

Dairy choices

- Milk substitutes: coconut, almond, cashew, flax, oat, rice, and soy milk, and so forth.

- Yogurt substitutes: cashew, coconut, almond, flax, and soy yogurts, and so on.

- Vegan cheddar: veggie-lover parmesan cheddar, destroyed and cut assortments, and so forth.

Egg choices

- aquafaba

- arrowroot powder

- chia seeds

- cornstarch

- flax dinner

- prepackaged veggie lover egg substitute

- silken tofu

Sound fats

- avocados
- avocado oil
- coconut oil
- flax oil
- olive oil
- unsweetened coconut
- tahini

Nibble nourishments

- edamame

- dark chocolate

- dried natural product

- fruit calfskin

- hummus

- nut spread

- pita chips

- popcorn

- roasted chickpeas

- seaweed crisps

- trail blend

Sugars

- coconut sugar

- dates

- maple syrup

- molasses

- monk natural product

- stevia

Flavors and toppings

- cayenne pepper

- chili powder

- cinnamon

- cumin

- garlic powder

- ground ginger

- nutritional yeast

- paprika

- pepper

- rosemary

- thyme

- turmeric

Note that many handled veggie-lover items found at the store —, for example, vegetarian meat substitutes — are regularly stacked with sodium, fillers, added substances, and different ingredients that may hurt your wellbeing.

Attempt to adhere to for the most part entire, natural nourishments — and avoid mock meats and other exceptionally prepared veggie-lover ingredients and premade suppers.

Rundown A decent vegetarian diet ought to incorporate a wide assortment of organic products, vegetables, entire grains, proteins, and solid fats.

Test supper plan

Here is an example one-week feast plan that highlights a couple of the nutritious nourishments that can be delighted in on a vegetarian diet.

Monday

- Breakfast: avocado, tempeh bacon with sautéed mushrooms, and withered arugula

- Lunch: entire grain pasta with lentil "meatballs" and a side serving of mixed greens

- Dinner: chickpea and cauliflower tacos with guacamole and pico de gallo

- Snacks: air-popped popcorn, kale chips, and trail blend

Tuesday

- Breakfast: coconut yogurt with berries, pecans, and chia seeds

- Lunch: prepared tofu with sautéed red cabbage, Brussels grows, and herbed couscous

- Dinner: mushroom lentil portion with garlic cauliflower and Italian green beans

- Snacks: chime peppers with guacamole, natural product calfskin, and ocean growth crisps

Wednesday

- Breakfast: sweet potato toast bested with nutty spread and banana

- Lunch: tempeh taco plate of mixed greens with quinoa, avocados, tomatoes, onions, beans, and cilantro

- Dinner: oat risotto with Swiss chard, mushrooms, and butternut squash

- Snacks: blended berries, veggie lover protein shake, and pecans

Thursday

- Breakfast: eggless quiche with smooth tofu, broccoli, tomatoes, and spinach

- Lunch: chickpea and spinach curry with dark-colored rice

- Dinner: Mediterranean lentil plate of mixed greens with cucumbers, olives, peppers, sun-dried tomatoes, kale, and parsley

- Snacks: cooked edamame, cut pear, and vitality balls produced using oats, chia seeds, nut spread, and dried organic product

Friday

- Breakfast: medium-term oats with apple cuts, pumpkin seeds, cinnamon, and nut spread

- Lunch: dark bean veggie burger with steamed broccoli and sweet potato wedges

- Dinner: macintosh and "cheddar" with healthful yeast and collard greens

- Snacks: pistachios, custom made granola, and coconut chia pudding

Saturday

- Breakfast: breakfast skillet with tempeh, broccoli, kale, tomatoes, and zucchini

- Lunch: garlic-ginger tofu with sautéed veggies and quinoa

- Dinner: bean plate of mixed greens with dark looked at peas, tomatoes, corn, chime peppers, and onions

- Snacks: cooked pumpkin seeds, solidified grapes, and celery with almond spread

Sunday

- Breakfast: entire grain toast with avocado and healthful yeast nearby a veggie-lover protein shake

- Lunch: lentil bean stew with flame-broiled asparagus and prepared potato

- Dinner: vegetable paella with dark colored rice, onions, tomatoes, chime peppers, artichoke, and chickpeas

• Snacks: almonds, natural product plate of mixed greens, and carrots with hummus

Synopsis The example dinner plan recorded above features a large number of the solid ingredients and dishes that can be delighted in on a balanced veggie lover diet.

7-Day Vegan Meal Plan: 1,200 Calories

Eating vegetarian is related to a diminished hazard for diabetes, coronary illness and particular sorts of disease. Also, at 1,200 calories, this veggie lover weight reduction feast plan sets you up to lose a solid 1 to 2 pounds every week.

Following a veggie lover diet, or even simply including more plant-based nourishments in your daily practice, can be a solid and scrumptious way to deal with eating. Research has indicated that reducing creature items and eating more beans, entire grains, natural products, vegetables, nuts and seeds are related to a diminished hazard for diabetes, coronary illness and specific kinds of disease. Also, you may have a simpler time getting thinner on a veggie lover diet, because of fiber-rich nourishments, which assist you with feeling full and fulfilled for the duration of the day.

At 1,200 calories, this vegetarian dinner plan sets you up to lose a sound 1 to 2 pounds every week and incorporates an assortment of nutritious nourishments and adjusted suppers to ensure you're getting the supplements you need every day. Regardless of whether you're a full-time veggie lover or simply searching for solid vegetarian formula thoughts, this plant-based feast plan makes for seven days of healthy eating.

The most effective method to Meal Prep You Week of Meals:

1. Make a group of the Vegan Pancakes to have for breakfast on Days 1, 5 and 7. Store the cooked hotcakes in a solitary layer in a water/air proof holder (To buy:amazon.com, $38) and solidify until prepared to eat; warm in the microwave.

2. Cook a group of Basic Quinoa to have for lunch on Day 2 and supper on Day 5.

3. Make the Quinoa and Chia Oatmeal Mix have on Day 4. Store the dry blend in an impenetrable holder (To buy:amazon.com, $17) for as long as a multi-month.

Day 1

Breakfast (296 calories)

- 2 Vegan Pancakes

- 1/4 cup blackberries

- 1 Tbsp. nutty spread

Blend nutty spread in with 1 tsp. warm water (or more, varying, to disperse the nutty spread). Sprinkle over hotcakes.

A.M. Bite (150 calories)

- 3/4 cup edamame units, prepared with a touch of salt

Lunch (245 calories)

- 1 serving White Bean and Avocado Toast

- 1 cup cut cucumber

P.M. Bite (30 calories)

- 1 little plum

Supper (499 calories)

- 1 serving Falafel Salad with Lemon-Tahini Dressing

Day by day Totals: 1,221 calories, 50 g protein, 137 g starches, 38 g fiber, 59 g fat, 1,586 mg sodium

Day 2

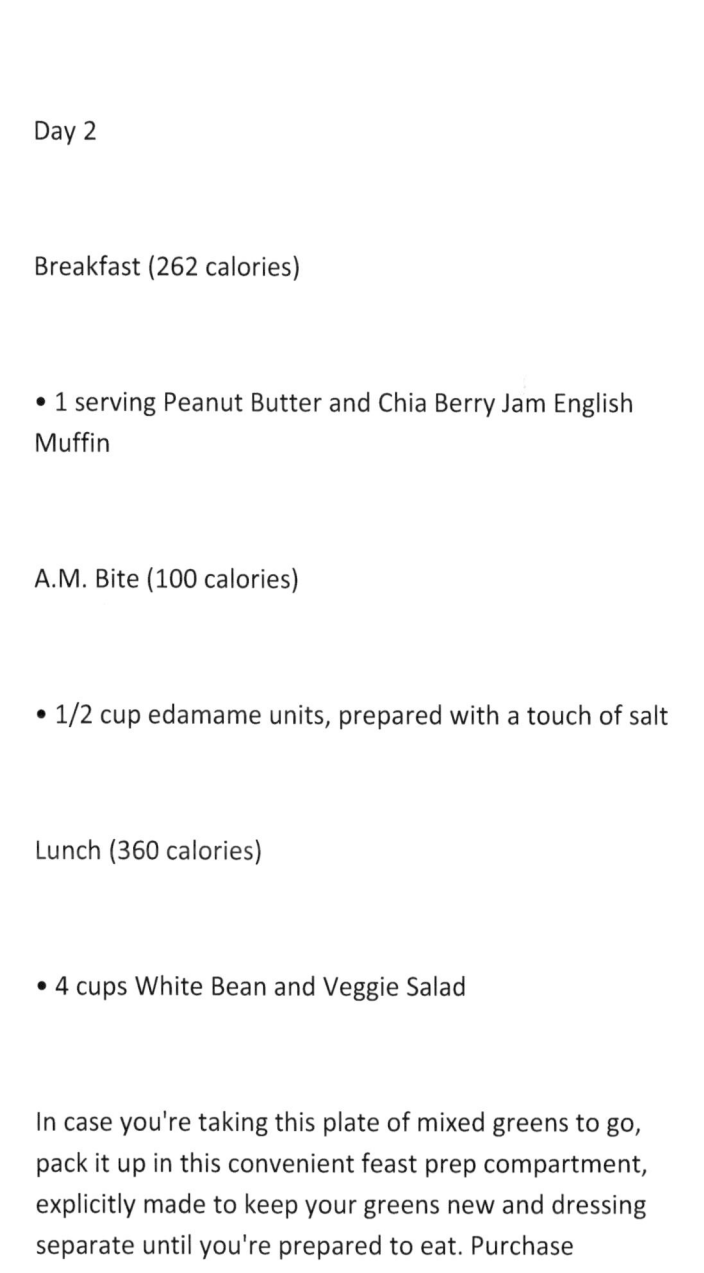

Breakfast (262 calories)

- 1 serving Peanut Butter and Chia Berry Jam English Muffin

A.M. Bite (100 calories)

- 1/2 cup edamame units, prepared with a touch of salt

Lunch (360 calories)

- 4 cups White Bean and Veggie Salad

In case you're taking this plate of mixed greens to go, pack it up in this convenient feast prep compartment, explicitly made to keep your greens new and dressing separate until you're prepared to eat. Purchase

It!amazon.com, $35 for a two-pack.

Supper (500 calories)

- 2 cups Black-Bean Quinoa Buddha Bowl

Day by day Totals: 1,220 calories, 48 g protein, 153 g starches, 46 g fiber, 53 g fat, 1,370 mg sodium

Day 3

Breakfast (266 calories)

- 1 serving Peanut Butter-Banana Toast

A.M. Tidbit (114 calories)

- 2 Tbsp. pumpkin seeds (pepitas)

Lunch (325 calories)

- 4 cups serving Green Salad with Edamame and Beets

P.M. Tidbit (62 calories)

- 2 cups air-popped popcorn

Supper (446 calories)

- 1 1/2 cups Roasted Cauliflower and Potato Curry Soup

- 1/2 little entire wheat pita, toasted

- 1/3 cup hummus

Feast Prep Tip: Save 1 serving of the Roasted Cauliflower and Potato Curry Soup in a watertight dinner prep holder (To buy:amazon.com, $7.19) for lunch on Day 4.

Day by day Totals: 1,213 calories, 49 g protein, 132 g starches, 34 g fiber, 57 g fat, 1,760 mg sodium

Day 4

Breakfast (296 calories)

- 1/3 cup Quinoa and Chia Oatmeal Mix cooked with 1/4 cups unsweetened soymilk

Feast Prep Tip: Make the Quinoa and Chia Oatmeal Mix and store in a sealed shut compartment for as long as a multi-month.

A.M. Tidbit (30 calories)

- 1 little plum

Lunch (309 calories)

- 1 1/2 cups Roasted Cauliflower and Potato Curry Soup

- 1/2 little entire wheat pita, toasted

P.M. Tidbit (114 calories)

- 2 Tbsp. pumpkin seeds (pepitas)

Supper (472 calories)

- 1 serving Stuffed Sweet Potato with Hummus Dressing

Day by day Totals: 1,222 calories, 51 g protein, 177 g starches, 40 g fiber, 40 g fat, 1,327 mg sodium

Day 5

Breakfast (296 calories)

- 2 Vegan Pancakes

- 1/4 cup blackberries

- 1 Tbsp. nutty spread

Blend nutty spread in with 1 tsp. warm water (or more, varying, to disperse the nutty spread). Sprinkle over hotcakes.

Lunch (325 calories)

- 1 serving Veggie and Hummus Sandwich

P.M. Bite (100 calories)

- 1/2 cup edamame units, prepared with a touch of salt

Supper (487 calories)

- 1 cup Chickpea Curry

- 1 cup Basic Quinoa

Day by day Totals: 1,208 calories, 44 g protein, 149 g starches, 33 g fiber, 50 g fat, 1,253 mg sodium

Day 6

Breakfast (262 calories)

- 1 serving Peanut Butter and Chia Berry Jam English Muffin

A.M. Bite (17 calories)

- 1/4 cup hummus

- 2 medium celery stalks, cut into sticks

Lunch (308 calories)

- 1 serving Vegan Bistro Lunch Box

- 2 Tbsp. pumpkin seeds (pepitas)

Supper (525 calories)

- 1 serving Thai Spaghetti Squash with Peanut Sauce

- 1 cup Vegan Thai Cucumber Salad

Day by day Totals: 1,211 calories, 51 g protein, 118 g sugars, 32 g fiber, 65 g fat, 2,065 mg sodium

Day 7

Breakfast (296 calories)

- 2 Vegan Pancakes

- 1/4 cup blackberries

- 1 Tbsp. nutty spread

Blend nutty spread in with 1 tsp. warm water (or more, varying, to disperse the nutty spread). Sprinkle over flapjacks.

A.M. Tidbit (62 calories)

- 1 medium orange

Lunch (325 calories)

- 4 cups serving Green Salad with Edamame and Beets

P.M. Tidbit (93 calories)

- 3 cups air-popped popcorn

Supper (434 calories)

- 1 serving Rainbow Veggie Spring Roll Bowl

Day by day Totals: 1,209 calories, 45 g protein, 144 g sugars, 32 g fiber, 51 g fat, 1,732 mg sodium

You Did It!

Congrats on completing this veggie lover weight reduction dinner plan. Possibly you tracked with each and every dinner and nibble or maybe simply utilized it as a persuasive guide for following a veggie lover diet. In any case, we trust you discovered this arrangement intriguing, flavorful and enlightening. Following a plant-based eating regimen dinner plan is a sound method to get in shape and keep it off. Keep doing awesome one of our other sound veggie lover dinner plans or vegan feast plans.

CHAPTER FOUR

Morning Recipes

1. Vegan fry-up

Nutrition: Per serving (two)

Kcal644

fat26g

saturates4g

carbs56g

sugars19g

fibre11g

protein41g

salt3.11grams

Ingredients

For Your hash browns

- 1 big potato
- , unpeeled
- 1 1/2 tablespoon peanut butter
- For the berries and mushrooms
- 14 cherry tomatoes
- jojoba oil
- 2 tsp walnut syrup
- 1 teaspoon soy sauce
- 1/4 tsp smoked paprika
- 1 large Portobello mushroom, sliced

- For Your scrambled tofu

- 349g pack silken tofu
- 2 tablespoon nutritional supplement

- 1/2 tsp turmeric

- 1 tsp garlic

- crushed

- To function

- 4 vegan sausages (we utilized Dee's leek & pumpkin)
- 1 x 200g can baked beans

Strategy

- Cook the curry entire in a big bowl of water, then simmers for 10 mins then drain and let it cool. Peel the skin off then coarsely grate. Mix using all the peanut butter and season well. Set aside in the refrigerator until needed.

- Heat the oven at 200C/180C fan/gas 6. Set the cherry tomatoes on a baking dish, drizzle with 2 tsp sunflower oil, season and bake for 30 mins or until the skins have blistered and begun to char. Cook the beans and simmer following the directions on the package so that they're prepared to function in precisely the exact same period as the scrambled tofu.

- Meanwhile, combine the maple syrup, soy sauce and 1/4 tsp smoked paprika together in a huge bowl, then add the chopped mushroom and toss to coat from the mix. Leave to stand as you pour two tsp sunflower oil to some non-stick skillet and bring this up into medium heat. Fry the mushroom till just beginning to turn gold but not charred. Twist onto a plate and keep warm before serving.

- Place 1 tablespoon oil to the skillet and then add spoonfuls of the potato mixture -- you ought to have about 4. Fry for 3-4 mins every side then squirt on kitchen paper.

- Crumble the tofu to your skillet and then scatter on the remaining ingredients along with a fantastic pinch of pepper and salt. If the pan seems a bit dry add a dab more oil. Fry for 3-4 mins or until the tofu is broken up into bits, nicely coated in the seasoning and warm through.

- Split everything between two plates and serve with a hot cup of tea produced with soy milk.

2. Coconut & banana sandwiches

Nutrition: per serving (10)

kcal179

fat8g

saturates6g

carbs23g

sugars11g

fibre1g

protein2g

salt0.2grams

Ingredients

- 150g plain flour
- 2 tsp coconut powder
- 3 tablespoons golden caster sugar
- 400ml may coconut milk, shaken well
- vegetable oil, for frying
- 1-2 bananas, thinly sliced
- 2 passion fruits, flesh scooped out

Technique

1. Sift the baking powder and flour into a bowl, and stir in 2 tablespoons of the sugar and a pinch of salt. Pour the coconut milk into a bowl, then whisk to combine in any fat that's split, then step out 300ml to a jug. Stir the milk gradually into the flour mixture to make a smooth

batter, then or whizz everything in a blender.

2. Heating A shallow skillet or flat griddle and brush it with oil. Use two tbsp of batter to create each pancake, skillet at a time -- some more will make it tricky to flip them. Push 4-5 parts of banana to each pancake and cook until bubbles begin to pop the surface, and the edges appear dry. They'll be a bit more fragile than egg-based pancakes, therefore turn them over carefully and cook another area for 1 minute. Duplicate to create 8-10 pancakes.

3. Meanwhile, Place the rest of the coconut milk and sugar in a small pan. Add a pinch of salt and simmer until the mixture thickens to the consistency of single cream. Use this as a sauce for that sausage and spoon over some of the flame seeds.

3. Vegan breakfast muffins

Nutrition: per serving

kcal224

fat 9g

saturates 1g

carbs 30g

sugars 15g

fibre 2g

protein 4g

salt 0.1grams

Ingredients

- 150g muesli mixture
- 50g light brown soft sugar
- 160g plain flour
- 1 teaspoon coconut powder

- 250ml sweetened soy milk
- 1 apple, peeled and grated

- 2 tbsp grapeseed oil

- 3 tablespoons nut butter (we utilized almond)

- 4 tablespoons demerara sugar

- 50g pecans, About chilled

Technique

1. Warming The stove to 200C/180C fan/gas 6. Line a biscuit tin with occasions. Blend 100g muesli in with the light-dark colored sugar, flour and heating powder in a bowl. Mix the milk, oil, apple and 2 tablespoons nut margarine in a container, at that point mix into the dry blend. Partition both between the conditions. Blend the rest of the muesli in with the demerara sugar remaining nut spread alongside the walnuts, and spoon over the cakes.

2. Heat For 25-30 mins or until the cakes are brilliant and rose. Will keep for a few days in a hermetically sealed compartment or suspend for a solitary month. Invigorate from the broiler before serving.

4. Cinnamon & blueberry French toast

Nutrition: per serving

kcal210

fat6g

saturates1g

carbs32g

sugars16g

fibre2g

protein5g

salt0.3grams

Ingredients

3 tablespoons walnut syrup

150g blueberries

2 tbsp gram flour

2 tbsp ground almonds

2 tsp cinnamon

200ml oat milk or milk milk

1 tablespoon golden caster sugar

1 teaspoon vanilla extract

6 pieces of thick white bread

Jojoba oil, for the frying pan

icing sugar for dusting

Technique

1. Gradually Warmth the maple syrup and blueberries in a saucepan until the berries begin to pop up and release their juices, and then place them to a side in the pan. Whisk the flour, almonds, cinnamon, vanilla and milk together in a shallow bowl.

2. Heating Just a little oil in a skillet. A piece of bread into the milk mixture, shake off any excess and fry the bread on both sides until it browns and crisps in the

borders. Keep the pieces warm in a very low oven since you cook the rest of the service with all the blueberries spooned over and dust with icing sugar.

5. Chive waffles with maple & soy mushrooms

Nutrition: per serving

- kcal227
- fat8g
- saturates1g
- carbs30g
- sugars7g
- fibre4g
- protein7g
- salt1.2grams

Ingredients

- 500ml soya milk or rice milk

1 teaspoon cider vinegar or lemon juice

2 tablespoon rapeseed oil

100g cooked, carrot sweet potato

150g polenta

130g plain yogurt

1 tablespoon coconut powder

little bunch chives snipped

1 tablespoon walnut syrup

2 tsp light soy sauce

6 big mushrooms

, thickly sliced

olive oil

, for frying

Soya yogurt, to serve (optional)

Technique

1. Heating the waffle iron. Mix the soya or rice milk together with all the vinegar and rapeseed oil (do not worry if it begins to divide), then dip in the sweet potato mash. Hint the polenta, flour and baking powder into a bowl, then combine and produce a well in the center. Add a large pinch of salt, then gradually pour in the milk mixture and whisk to make a batter. Stir in half the chives.

2. Pour enough batter into the waffle iron to fill and cook for 4-5 mins. Lift the waffle, keep it warm and repeat with the remaining mix till you've got six waffles.

3. Meanwhile, combine the maple syrup using the soy

sauce. Brush it on the mushrooms and season with pepper. Heat a little oil in a skillet and fry the mushrooms on either side till they are browned and cooked through -- be sure they don't burn the borders. Serve the waffles topped with mushrooms, then add a spoonful of soya yogurt, if you prefer, and scatter over the remaining chives.

6. Tofu brekkie pancakes

Nutrition: per serving (6)

- kcal377
- fat14g
- saturates2g
- carbs47g
- sugars21g
- fibre7g
- protein12g
- salt1.6grams

Ingredients

50g Brazil nuts

3 chopped tsp

240g raspberries

maple syrup or honey, to function

For your batter

349g pack firm silken tofu

2 tsp vanilla extract

2 tsp lemon juice

400ml unsweetened almond milk

1 tablespoon vegetable oil, also 1-2 tbsp extra for frying pan

250g buckwheat flour

4 tablespoons light muscovado sugar

11/2 tsp ground mixed spice

1 tablespoon fermented coconut powder

Technique

1. Heating Oven to 180C/160C fan/gas 4. Scatter the nuts above a skillet and cook for 5 mins until toasty and gold. Leave to cool, then chop. Turn the oven down if you would like to maintain the entire batch of sausage hot, although I believe that they are best enjoyed right from the pan.

2. Place the carrot, vanilla, lemon juice along with 200ml of this milk into a profound jug or jar. Using a stick blender, mix together till liquid, keep moving until it turns smooth and thick, such as yogurt. Stir in the oil and the remainder of the milk to loosen the mix.

3. Place the dry ingredients and 1 teaspoon salt in a large bowl and whisk to blend and aerate. Whether there aren't any lumps in the glucose squish them together with your palms. Create a well in the middle, pour into the carrot mixture and deliver together to make a thick batter.

4. Heating A large (ideally none) skillet and swirl about

1 teaspoon oil. For gold pancakes that don't adhere, the oil and pan ought to be hot enough to find an enthusiastic sizzle connected with the batter, but not too hot it scorches it. Test a fall.

5. Utilizing A ladle or large serving spoon, fall in 3 spoonfuls of batter, then relieving out it softly in the pan to make pancakes which are about 12cm across. Cook for 2 mins on the initial side until bubbles pop over the majority of the surface. Loosen using a palette knife, then flip on the sandwiches and cook for 1 minute until puffed up and company. Transfer into the oven to stay warm, if you want to, but do not pile the pancakes too tightly. Cook the rest of the batter, with a bit more oil every time. Serve warm with chopped banana, berries, toasted nuts and a fantastic drizzle of maple syrup or honey.

7. Cardamom & walnut quinoa porridge

Nutrition: per serving

kcal231

fat4g

saturates1g

carbs37g

sugars10g

fibre6g

protein8g

salt0.2grams

Cardamom & peach quinoa porridge

Serves 2

A wholesome breakfast of oats and quinoa with new ripe peach. Almond milk leaves its appropriate for dairy-free and vegetarian diets

Healthy

Vegetarian

Vegan

Nutrition: per serving

kcal231

fat4g

saturates1g

carbs37g

sugars10g

fibre6g

protein8g

salt0.2grams

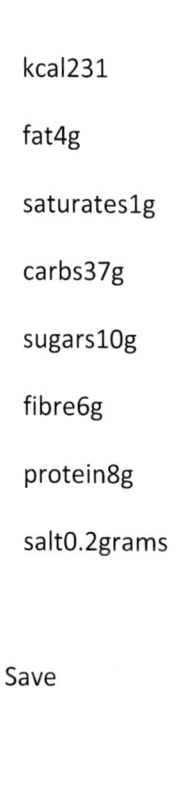

Save

Printing

Ingredients

- 75g quinoa
- 25g porridge oats
- 4 cardamom pods

250ml unsweetened almond milk

2 ripe peaches, cut into pieces

1 teaspoon walnut syrup

Technique

1. Place the quinoa, ginger and cardamom pods in a little saucepan with 250ml water along with 100ml of this almond milk. Bring to the boil, then simmer gently for 15 mins, stirring periodically.

2. Pour From the residual almond milk and cook for 5 mins longer until creamy.

3. Eliminate That the cardamom pods, spoon into jars or bowls, and shirt with all the berry and maple syrup.

8. Protein pancakes

Nutrition: per serving

kcal798

fat32g

saturates8g

carbs91g

sugars39g

fibre15g

protein29g

salt0.3grams

Ingredients

For Your batter

- 2 tbsp ground flaxseeds
- 20g floor peppers
- 300ml soya milk
- 200g quinoa flour

- 1 moderate banana

, mashed

2 tablespoon walnut syrup

coconut oil, for frying

For your blueberry chia jam (leaves 200ml)

200g blueberries

, mashed

2 tablespoon chia seeds

1-2 tablespoon walnut syrup

, to taste

2 tsp lemon juice

For your pile

100g coconut milk or Greek yogurt

1 tablespoon pistachio nuts or pumpkin seeds, sliced, toasted if you prefer

2 tbsp hulled hemp seeds

mixed berries

Technique

1. In A small bowl stir the flaxseeds using 6 tablespoons water and set aside to soak as you make the shake.

2. Mash the tomatoes using a fork at a pan then place above a low-medium heat until syrupy and bubbling. Take off the heat and stir in the chia seeds, maple syrup and lemon juice. Leave to cool slightly then move to a little serving jar.

3. Place the ground almonds, milk, flour, banana, maple

syrup and a pinch of salt in a blender. Stir the carrot to be certain it is now thick and gloopy, such as an egg, then tip in the mixture and blitz until thick and smooth.

4. Heating 1 teaspoon of coconut oil in a large skillet over a moderate heat and add tbsp dollops of batter to the pan. Cook for a few mins on one side before the edges are browning, and bubbles have formed on top. When the light, white batter has turned into a sandy color, flip over using a spatula and cook for a few mins till dark golden brown. Set aside and keep warm as you repeat the procedure with the remaining batter, adding a different teaspoon of coconut oil with every batch. You need to make about 16 pancakes.

5. Pile The sausage high between 2 plates, alternating the layers together with spoonfuls of jam and yogurt. Dollop any leftover yogurt and a spoonful of jam in addition to scattering over the nuts, berries and seeds to function. The leftover jam will keep in the refrigerator for up to 1 week.

9. Blackcurrant compote

Nutrition: per serving

kcal15

fat0g

saturates0g

carbs3g

sugars3g

fibre1g

protein0g

salt0g

Ingredients

juice 1/2 lemon

500g blackcurrants

100g golden caster sugar

Technique

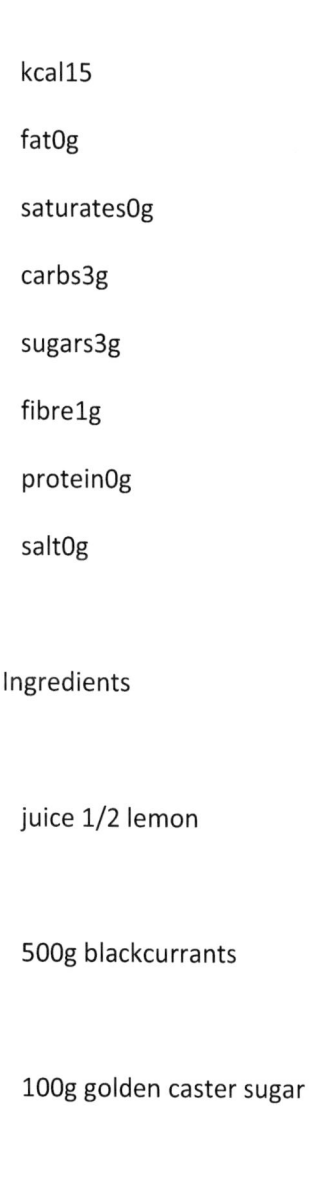

1. Place 2 tablespoons water and the lemon juice in a large saucepan, bring to the boil, then put in the blackcurrants and simmer till broken down.

2. Hint From the golden caster sugar and deliver about 105C on a temperature probe. Pour into sterilized jars and leave to cool. Will keep in the refrigerator for up to 3 months.

10. Green rainbow berry bowl

Nutrition: per serving

kcal251

fat16g

saturates3g

carbs19g

sugars18g

fibre7g

protein4g

salt 0.2grams

Ingredients

50g spinach

1 avocado

, stoned, peeled and halved

1 ripe pear, stoned, peeled and cut into balls

1 apple, cored and cut into chunks

200ml almond milk

1 dragon fruit, peeled and slice to chunks

100g mixed berries (we utilized berries, blueberries and raspberries)

Technique

1. Place the spinach, cherry, cherry, apple and almond milk in a blender, and blitz until thick and smooth. Split between 2 bowls and top with the dragon berries and fruit.

11. Raspberry ripple chia pudding

Nutrition: per serving

kcal257

fat10g

saturates3g

carbs26g

sugars22g

fibre13g

protein8g

salt0.2grams

Ingredients

50g white chia seeds

200ml coconut drinking milk

1 nectarine

Or walnut, cut into pieces

2 tablespoon goji berries

For your raspberry purée

100g raspberries

1 teaspoon lemon juice

2 tsp walnut syrup

Technique

1. Split The chia seeds and almond milk involving 2 serving bowls and stir well. Leave to boil for 5 mins, stirring occasionally, until the seeds swell and thicken when awakened.

2. Meanwhile, Blend the purée components in a small food processor, or blitz using a hand blender. Swirl a spoonful into each bowl, then organize the nectarine or peach slices on top and scatter the goji berries. I will keep in the refrigerator for 1 day. Insert the toppings just prior to serving.

12. Tropical smoothie

Nutrition: per serving

kcal332

fat15g

saturates13g

carbs41g

sugars38g

fibre8g

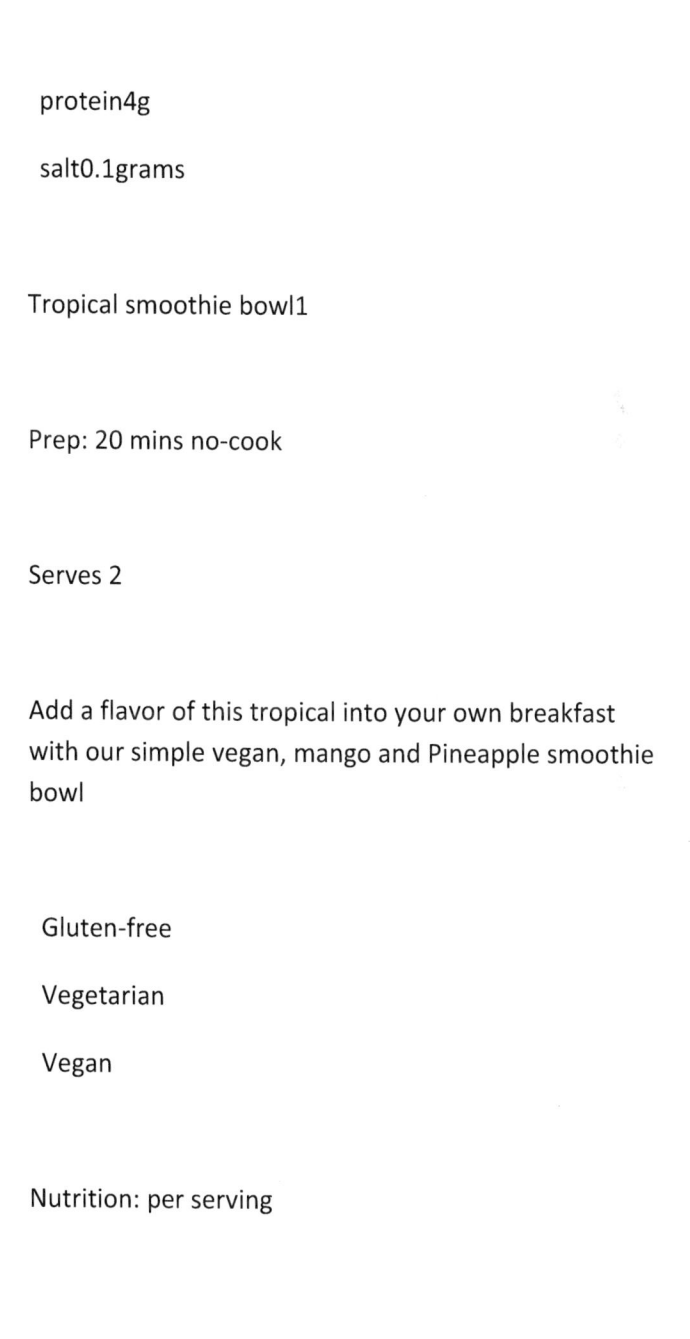

protein 4g

salt 0.1grams

Tropical smoothie bowl 1

Prep: 20 mins no-cook

Serves 2

Add a flavor of this tropical into your own breakfast with our simple vegan, mango and Pineapple smoothie bowl

- Gluten-free
- Vegetarian
- Vegan

Nutrition: per serving

kcal332

fat15g

saturates13g

carbs41g

sugars38g

fibre8g

protein4g

salt0.1grams

Ingredients

1 small ripe pear, stoned, peeled and cut into balls

200g pineapple

, peeled, cored and cut into chunks

2 ripe tsp

2 tablespoons coconut milk (not coconut-flavored yogurt)

150ml coconut drinking milk

2 passion fruits, halved, seeds scooped out

handful blueberries

2 tablespoons coconut scents

a few mint leaves

Technique

1. Place The cherry, pineapple, bananas, yogurt and coconut milk in a blender, and blitz until thick and smooth. Pour into two bowls and decorate with all the passion fruit, blueberries, coconut flakes and mint leaves. I will keep in the refrigerator for 1 day. Insert the toppings just prior to serving.

13. Summer porridge

Nutrition: per serving

kcal391

fat12g

saturates2g

carbs49g

sugars19g

fibre14g

protein14g

salt0.2grams

Ingredients

300ml almond milk

200g blueberries

1/2 tablespoon walnut syrup

2 tbsp chia seeds

100g jumbo oats

1 kiwi berry

, cut into pieces

50g pomegranate seeds

2 tsp mixed seeds

Technique

1. In A blender, blitz the milk, blueberries and maple syrup before the milk turns purple. Place the chia and oats at a mixing bowl, then pour into the skillet and stir really well. Leave to boil for 5 mins, stirring occasionally, until the liquid has consumed, along with the oats and chia swell and thicken.

2. Stir Again, then split between 2 bowls. Arrange the fruit on top, and then scatter over the seeds that are mixed. I will keep in the refrigerator for 1 day. Insert the toppings just prior to serving.

14. Vegan tomato & coriander pancakes

Nutrition: per serving

kcal609

fat35g

saturates4g

carbs59g

sugars6g

fibre6g

protein18g

salt0.87grams

Ingredients

140g white self-raising flour

1 teaspoon soy flour

400ml soya milk

vegetable oil, for frying pan

For the topping

2 tablespoons vegetable oil

250g button mushrooms

250g cherry tomatoes halved

2 tablespoon soy cream or soya milk

sizable number pine nuts

snipped chives, to function

Technique

1. Sift the flours along with a pinch of salt into a blender. Add the soya milk and mix to create a smooth batter.

2. Heating Just a little oil in a moderate non-stick skillet till very hot. Pour about 3 tablespoons of the batter to the pan and cook over moderate heat until bubbles

appear on the surface of the pancake. Flip the pancake over with a palette knife and cook on the other side until golden brown. Repeat with the remaining batter, keeping the cooked pancakes warm as you move. You may make roughly 8.

3. For the topping, heat the oil in a skillet. Cook the mushrooms until tender, then add the tomatoes and cook for a few mins. Pour from the soya cream or milk and pine nuts, then cook till blended. Split the sausage between two plates, then spoon on the berries and mushrooms. Scatter with chives.

15. Vegan granola

Nutrition: per serving

kcal407

fat26g

saturates12g

carbs34g

sugars12g

fibre5g

protein 8g

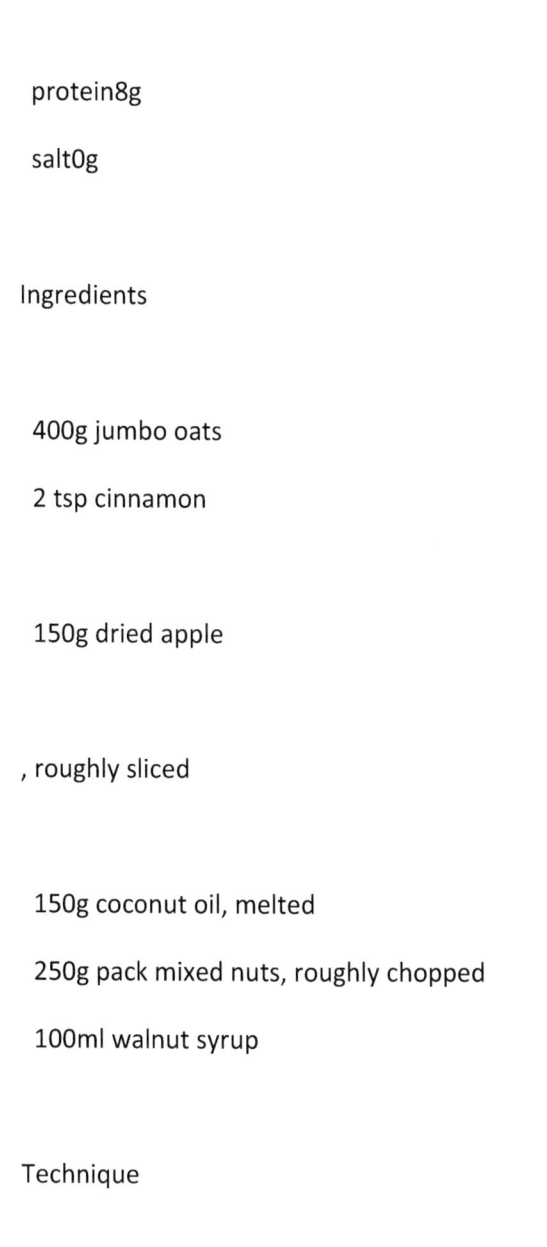

salt 0g

Ingredients

- 400g jumbo oats
- 2 tsp cinnamon
- 150g dried apple, roughly sliced
- 150g coconut oil, melted
- 250g pack mixed nuts, roughly chopped
- 100ml walnut syrup

Technique

1. Warming Oven to 180C/160C fan/gas 4. Line two enormous preparing plates with heating material. Combine the entirety of the ingredients with the exception of the maple syrup. Spread the granola out onto the plate and shower over the maple syrup.

2. Heat From the stove for 20 mins, mixing the granola pleasantly part of the way through so it cooks equally. Leave to cool before putting away in a Kilner container or hermetically sealed holder. Best eaten inside multi-month.

16. Mexican beans & avocado toast

Nutrition: per serving

kcal368

fat19g

saturates3g

carbs30g

sugars6g

fibre13g

protein12g

salt 0.9grams

Ingredients

270g cherry tomatoes, quartered

1 white or red onion

, finely chopped

1/2 lime

, juiced

4 tablespoons olive oil

2 garlic cloves, crushed

1 teaspoon ground cumin

2 tsp chipotle paste or 1 tsp chili flakes

2 x 400g cans black beans, drained

little bunch coriander, chopped

4 slices bread

1 avocado, finely chopped

Strategy

1. Mix the berries, 1/4 onion, lime juice and 1 tablespoon oil and set aside. Fry the remaining onion in 2 tablespoons oil until it begins to soften. Add the garlic, fry for 1 minute, then add the cumin and chipotle and stir fry until aromatic. Hint in the legumes and a dash of water, cook and stir gently until heated through. Stir in the majority of the tomato mixture and cook 1 minute, season well and include the majority of the coriander.

2. Toast the bread and garnish with the remaining 1 tablespoon oil. Set a piece on each plate and pile a few beans on top. Organize some pieces of avocado on top, and then scatter the remaining tomato mixture and coriander leaves to function.

17. Three-grain porridge

Nutrition: per serving

kcal 179

fat 2g

saturates 0g

carbs 32g

sugars 1g

fibre 4g

protein 7g

salt 0g

Three-grain porridge

Serves 18

This Nutritious breakfast, made from toasted oatmeal, barley and wheat, is Super easy to create and may be maintained for up to six months

Healthy

Vegetarian

Vegan

Nutrition: per serving

kcal 179

fat 2g

saturates 0g

carbs 32g

sugars 1g

fibre 4g

protein 7g

salt 0g

Ingredients

300g oatmeal

300g spelled flakes

300g barley flakes

agave nectar and chopped strawberries, to serve (optional)

Technique

1. Working in batches, toast the oatmeal, spelled flakes and barley at a big, dry skillet for 5 mins until golden, then leave to cool and store in an airtight container.

2. When You would like to consume that, just blend 50g of this porridge mix in a saucepan with 300ml water or milk. Cook for 5 mins, stirring occasionally, then top with a spoonful of honey and tomatoes, if you prefer (optional). It will keep for 6 weeks.

18. Sunshine smoothie

Nutrition: per serving

kcal171

fat4g

saturates 1g

carbs 30g

sugars 27g

fibre 3g

protein 3g

salt 0.2grams

Ingredients

500ml lettuce

juice, chilled

200g pineapple (canned or fresh)

Two bananas, broken into chunks

Little piece ginger, peeled

20g cashew nuts juice lime

Technique

1. Place The ingredients at a blender and whizz until smooth. Drink directly away or pour into a jar to drink on the move. Will keep in the refrigerator for a single day.

19. Vegan smoothie

Nutrition: per serving

kcal186

fat5g

saturates1g

carbs25g

sugars16g

fibre3g

protein9g

salt0.1grams

Ingredients

100ml (1/4 tall glass) cherry

Juice (we utilized Cherrygood)

200ml (1/2 tall glass) unsweetened soya milk

1 cherry soya yogurt

3 tablespoons or 50g firm silken tofu

75g (1 vacant yogurt kettle) frozen cherry

2 tbsp porridge oat

Technique

1. Quantify each of the components just or utilize a tall glass along with your empty yogurt pot for rate -- they do not need to be precise. Place them in a blender and blitz until smooth. Pour 1 tall glass (you will have enough to get a high up) or 2 short tumblers.

20. Kiwi fruit smoothie

Nutrition: per serving (3)

kcal163

fat1g

saturates0.1grams

carbs36g

sugars35g

fibre3g

protein2g

salt0.04grams

Ingredients

3 peeled kiwi berry

1 mango, peeled, stoned and sliced

500ml lemon juice

1 banana

, sliced

Strategy

1. Place all the ingredients at a blender and blitz until smooth then pour into two tall glasses.

21. Raw strawberry shake

Nutrition: per tablespoon

kcal12

fat0.3grams

saturates0g

carbs2g

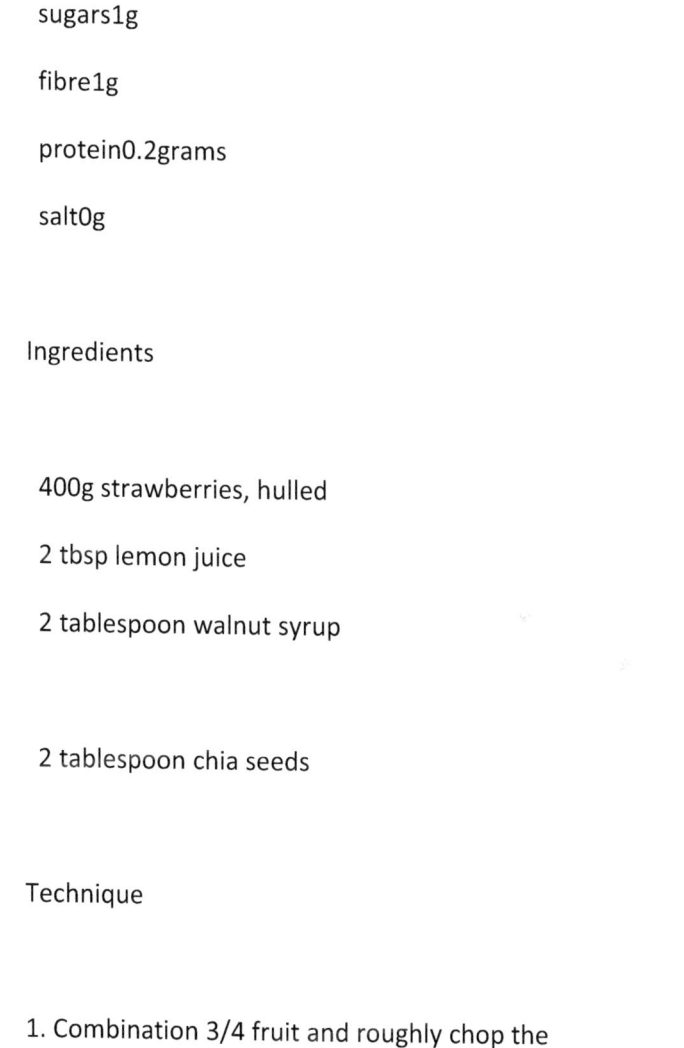

sugars1g

fibre1g

protein0.2grams

salt0g

Ingredients

400g strawberries, hulled

2 tbsp lemon juice

2 tablespoon walnut syrup

2 tablespoon chia seeds

Technique

1. Combination 3/4 fruit and roughly chop the remainder. Insert the remaining ingredients blend well and leave for 1 hr, stirring occasionally, until thickened. Shop in a sterilized jar in the refrigerator for up to 4 days or freeze up to 1 month.

Ingredients

400g strawberries, hulled

2 tbsp lemon juice

2 tablespoon walnut syrup

2 tablespoon chia seeds

Technique

1. Combination 3/4 fruit and roughly chop the remainder. Insert the remaining ingredients blend well and leave for 1 hr, stirring occasionally, until thickened. Shop in a sterilized jar in the refrigerator for up to 4 days or freeze up to 1 month.

22. Pistachio & cardamom butter

Nutrition: per tablespoon

kcal87

fat 7g

saturates 1g

carbs 3g

sugars 1g

fibre 2g

protein 3g

salt 0.1grams

Ingredients

- 10 cardamom pods
- 400g pistachio nut kernels
- 1 tablespoon walnut syrup
- 1/2 tsp sea salt flakes
- 2-3 tsp groundnut oil

Technique

1. Eliminate The seeds from the cardamom pods and finely crush them in a pestle and mortar.

2. Hint The nuts into a food processor, add the crushed cardamom, maple syrup and salt. Blend for 7-8 mins, till you are left with nut butter to loosen the consistency, then add a spoonful of oil and mix again.

23. Orange & mint salad

Nutrition: per serving

- kcal222
- fat1g
- saturates0g
- carbs54g
- sugars54g
- fibre5g
- protein4g
- salt0.04grams

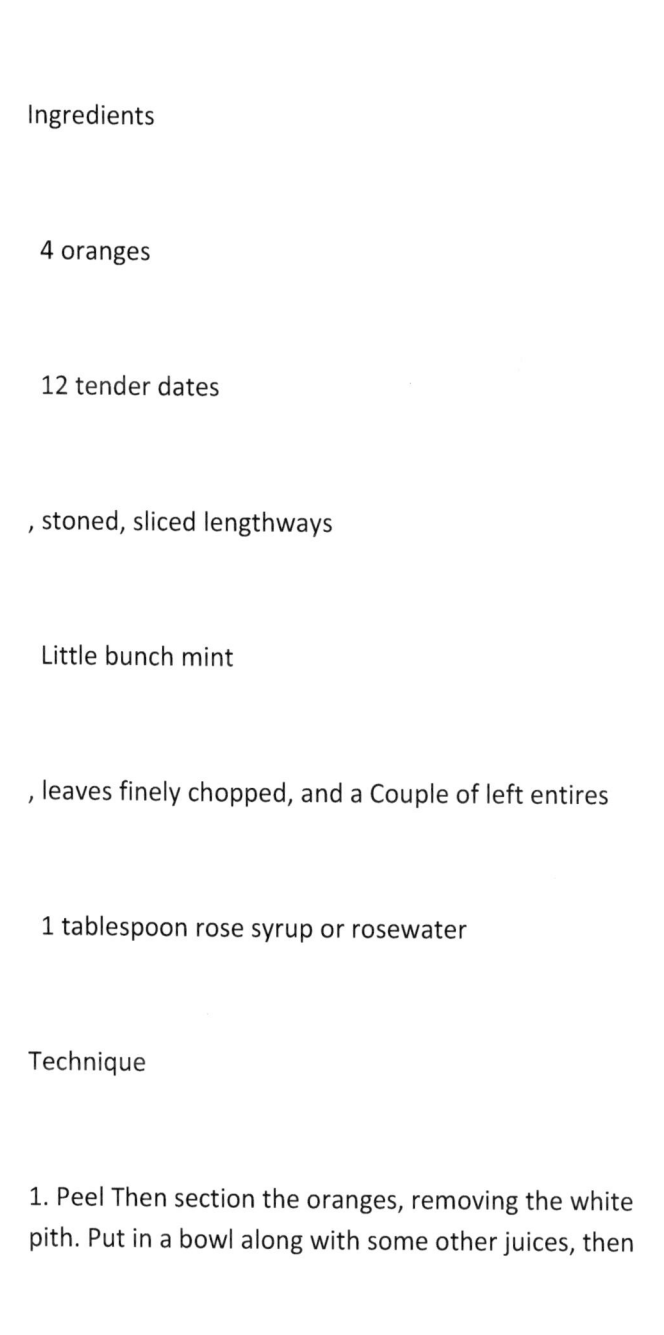

Ingredients

4 oranges

12 tender dates, stoned, sliced lengthways

Little bunch mint, leaves finely chopped, and a Couple of left entires

1 tablespoon rose syrup or rosewater

Technique

1. Peel Then section the oranges, removing the white pith. Put in a bowl along with some other juices, then

add the dates, chopped mint and rose syrup and toss lightly. Split between 4 dessert bowls, then scatter the mint leaves and serve.

24. Creamy strawberry & coconut smoothie

Nutrition: per serving

kcal212

fat11g

saturates7g

carbs22g

sugars19g

fibre3g

protein4g

salt0.11grams

Ingredients

200ml (1/2 tall glass) coconut milk

(we utilized Kara Dairy Free)

4 tablespoons coconut milk yogurt

(we utilized Coyo)

1 banana

1 tablespoon ground flaxseed, sunflower and pumpkin seed (we utilized Linwoods)

120g (1/4 bag) frozen mango chunks

1 passion fruit, to complete (optional)

Technique

1. Quantify each of the components or utilize a tall glass for rate -- they do not need to be precise. Place them in a blender and blitz until smooth. Pour 1 tall glass (you will have enough to get a high up) or 2 short tumblers.

Cut the passion fruit in half, if using, then scrape the seeds in addition.

25. Grapefruit, agave & pistachio salad

Nutrition: per serving

kcal107

fat1g

saturates0g

carbs21g

sugars12g

fibre2g

protein2g

salt0g

Ingredients

1 pink strawberry

1 whitened grapefruit

1 tablespoon agave nectar

1 teaspoon chopped pistachio

Technique

1. Segment Grapefruits, eliminating as much of the pith as possible. Split the sections Between 2 bowls and top with agave and pistachios.

CHAPTER FIVE

Lunch Recipes

1. Vegetarian banh mi

Sustenance: Per serving

kcal338

fat11g

saturates0g

carbs40g

sugars7g

fibre7g

protein 16g

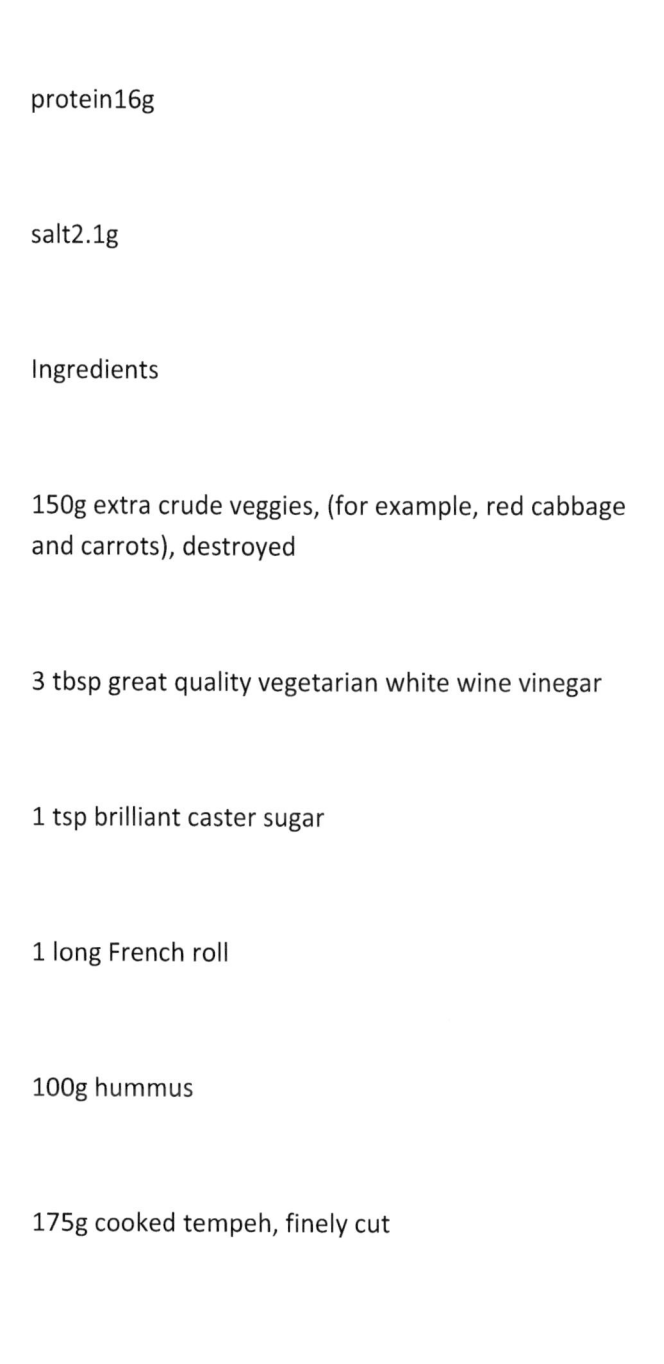

salt 2.1g

Ingredients

150g extra crude veggies, (for example, red cabbage and carrots), destroyed

3 tbsp great quality vegetarian white wine vinegar

1 tsp brilliant caster sugar

1 long French roll

100g hummus

175g cooked tempeh, finely cut

½ little pack coriander, leaves picked, to serve

½ little pack mint, leaves picked, to serve

hot sauce, to serve (we utilized sriracha)

Technique

1. Put the destroyed veg in a bowl and include the vinegar, sugar and 1 tsp salt. Hurl everything together, at that point put aside to pickle rapidly while you set up the remainder of the sandwich.

1. Heat broiler to 180C/160C fan/gas 4. Cut the loaf into four, at that point cut each piece on a level plane down the middle. Put the loaf pieces in the broiler for 5 mins until daintily toasted and warm. Spread each piece with a layer of hummus, at that point top four pieces with the tempeh cuts and heap the salted veg on top. To serve, sprinkle over the herbs and press over some hot sauce, at that point top with the other loaf pieces to make sandwiches.

2. 'Cheesy' veggie-lover scones

Nourishment: Per serving

kcal235

fat6g

saturates1g

carbs35g

sugars1g

fibre3g

protein8g

salt 1g

Ingredients

3 tbsp olive oil, in addition to extra for the plate

1 tsp white wine vinegar

250ml almond milk

1 cauliflower stalk (around 100g)

300g self-raising flour, in addition to extra for cleaning

½ tsp preparing powder

3 tbsp dietary yeast

¼ tsp mustard powder

¼ tsp smoked paprika

3 thyme sprigs, leaves picked

veggie lover onion chutney, to serve

Strategy

1. Warmth stove to 220C/200C fan/gas 7 and gently oil a heating plate. Blend the vinegar in with the almond milk and put it in a safe spot. Carry a pot of water to the bubble, include the cauliflower stalk and cook for 5 mins until practically delicate. Channel well, leave to cool, at that point finely hack.

2. Blend the flour, preparing powder, nourishing yeast, flavors, thyme leaves and 1 tsp salt in an enormous bowl. Include the cauliflower, at that point, include the oil and pour in 230ml of the soured almond milk. Working rapidly, unite the blend with a wooden spoon;

if there is any dry blend in the bowl, add more almond milk to make a delicate yet not clingy mixture. Tip the batter onto a floured work surface and pat to a thickness of about 2.5cm. Cut out rounds with a 6cm fluted shaper and move to the preparing plate. Assemble any offcuts and cut out more adjusts.

3. Bake on the first-rate of the broiler for 10-12 mins until brilliant. Serve warm with onion chutney.

2. Bean, tomato and watercress plate of mixed greens

Nourishment: Per serving

kcal454

fat23g

saturates3g

carbs40g

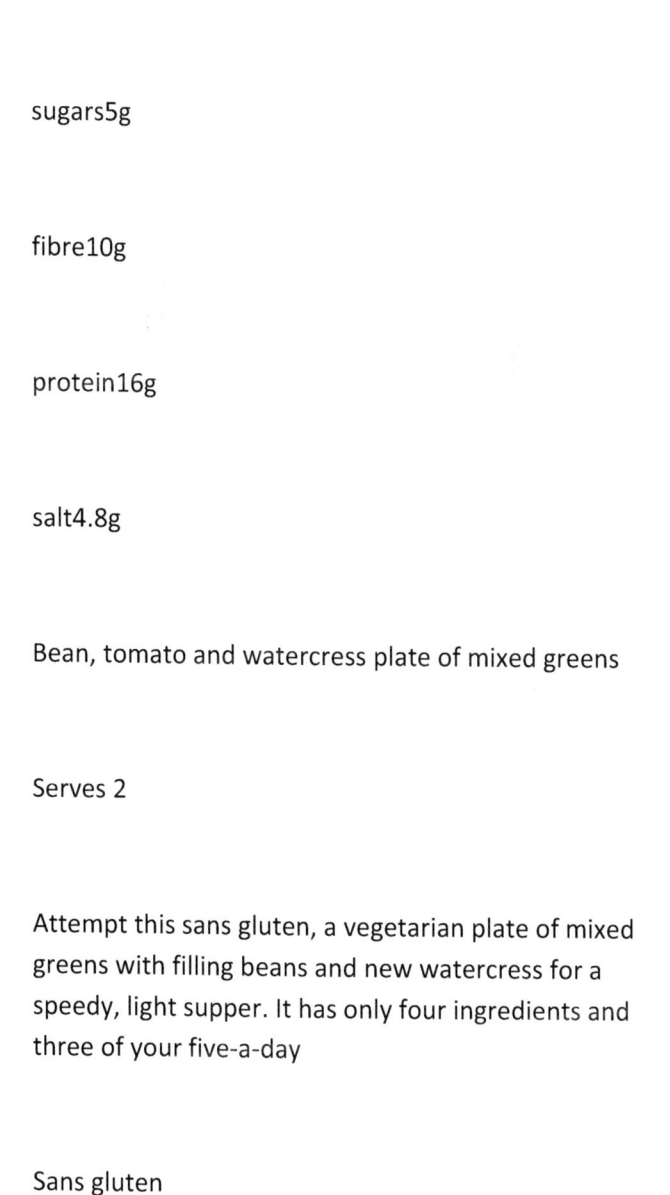

sugars5g

fibre10g

protein16g

salt4.8g

Bean, tomato and watercress plate of mixed greens

Serves 2

Attempt this sans gluten, a vegetarian plate of mixed greens with filling beans and new watercress for a speedy, light supper. It has only four ingredients and three of your five-a-day

Sans gluten

Vegan

Vegetarian

Sustenance: Per serving

kcal 454

fat 23g

saturates 3g

carbs 40g

sugars 5g

fibre 10g

protein 16g

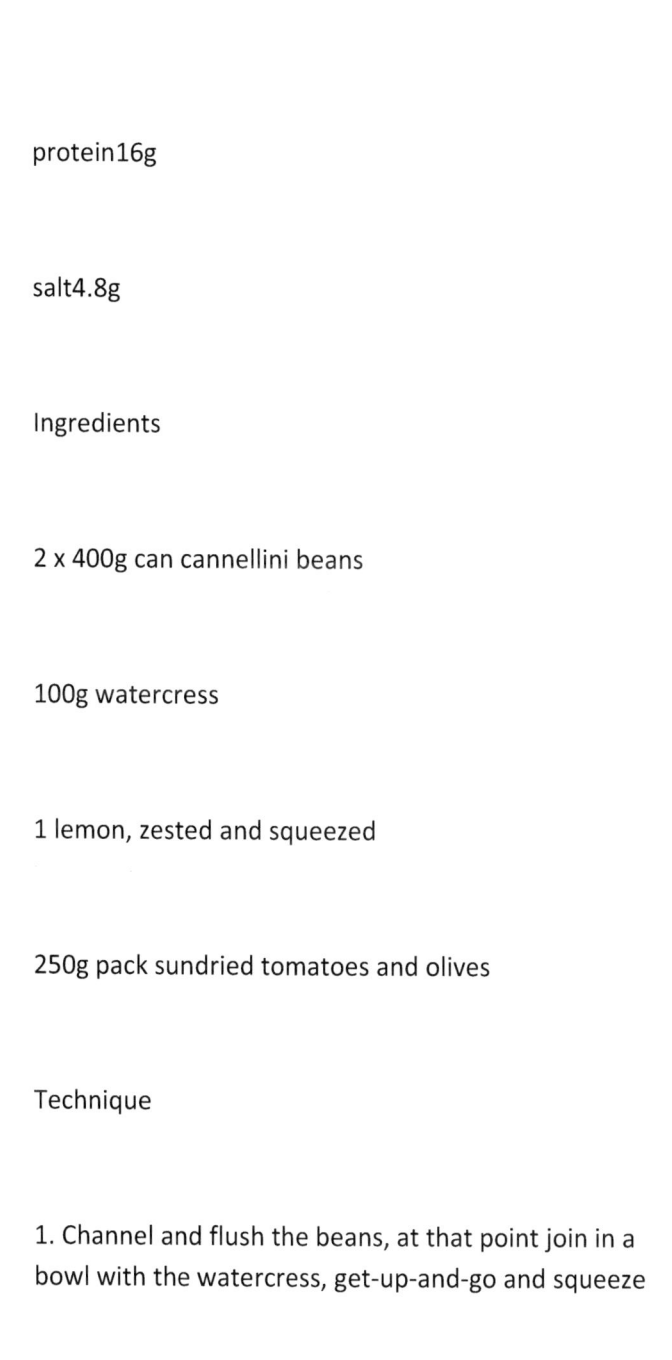

salt 4.8g

Ingredients

2 x 400g can cannellini beans

100g watercress

1 lemon, zested and squeezed

250g pack sundried tomatoes and olives

Technique

1. Channel and flush the beans, at that point join in a bowl with the watercress, get-up-and-go and squeeze

of the lemon, tomatoes and olives, including the oil from the pack. Hurl well and season to taste.

4. Vegan chickpea curry coat potatoes

Sustenance: Per serving

kcal276

fat9g

saturates3g

carbs32g

sugars12g

fibre11g

protein 12g

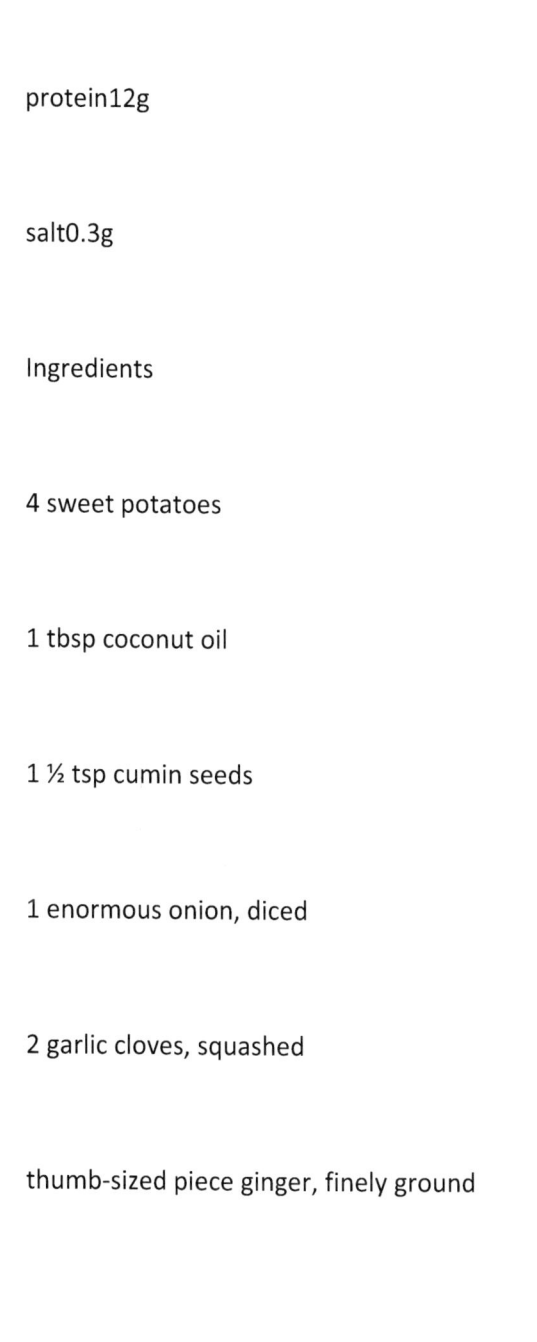

salt 0.3g

Ingredients

4 sweet potatoes

1 tbsp coconut oil

1 ½ tsp cumin seeds

1 enormous onion, diced

2 garlic cloves, squashed

thumb-sized piece ginger, finely ground

1 green bean stew, finely slashed

1 tsp garam masala

1 tsp ground coriander

½ tsp turmeric

2 tbsp tikka masala glue

2 x 400g can slash tomatoes

2 x 400g can chickpeas, depleted

Lemon wedges and coriander leaves, to serve

Technique

1. Warmth broiler to 200C/180C fan/gas 6. Prick the sweet potatoes done with a fork, at that point put on a heating plate and meal in the stove for 45 mins or until delicate when penetrated with a blade.

2. In the interim, dissolve the coconut oil in a huge pot over medium warmth. Include the cumin seeds and fry for 1 min until fragrant, at that point include the onion and fry for 7-10 mins until relaxed.

3. Put the garlic, ginger and green bean stew into the dish, and cook for 2-3 mins. Include the flavors and tikka masala glue and cook for a further 2 mins until fragrant, at that pointed tip in the tomatoes. Bring to a stew, at that pointed tip in the chickpeas and cook for a further 20 mins until thickened. Season.

4. Put the broiled sweet potatoes on four plates and cut open lengthways. Spoon over the chickpea curry and crush over the lemon wedges. Season, at that point disperse with coriander before serving.

5. Beetroot and lentil tabbouleh

kcal 346

fat 15g

saturates 2g

carbs 35g

sugars 7g

fibre 11g

protein 13g

salt 0.3g

Ingredients

1 little pack level leaf parsley, in addition to adding leaves to serve (discretionary)

1 little pack mint

1 little pack chives

200g radishes

2 beetroot, stripped and quartered

1 red apple, cored, quartered and cut

1 tsp ground cumin

4 tbsp olive oil

250g pack cooked quinoa

400g can chickpeas, depleted and washed

400g can green lentils, depleted

2 lemons, juiced

Strategy

1. Put the herbs, radishes and beetroot in a nourishment processor and rush until cleaved into little pieces. Mix in the remainder of the ingredients, including the lemon squeeze a piece at once to taste – you may not require every last bit of it. Season, at that point place on a huge platter beat with a couple of parsley leaves, in the event that you like, and serve straight away.

6.Meze bento

Nourishment: Per serving

kcal 520

fat 22g

saturates 1g

carbs 57g

sugars 11g

fibre 18g

protein 14g

salt 3.1g

Ingredients

2 tbsp hummus

bunch of olives

1 cut wholemeal pitta

1 hacked carrot

1 hacked infant fennel bulb

2-3 instant stuffed vine leaves

4 tbsp tabbouleh

Strategy

1. Put 2 tbsp hummus in a compartment in a bento box. Fill different areas with other meze ingredients – we utilized a bunch of olives, 1 cut wholemeal pitta, 1

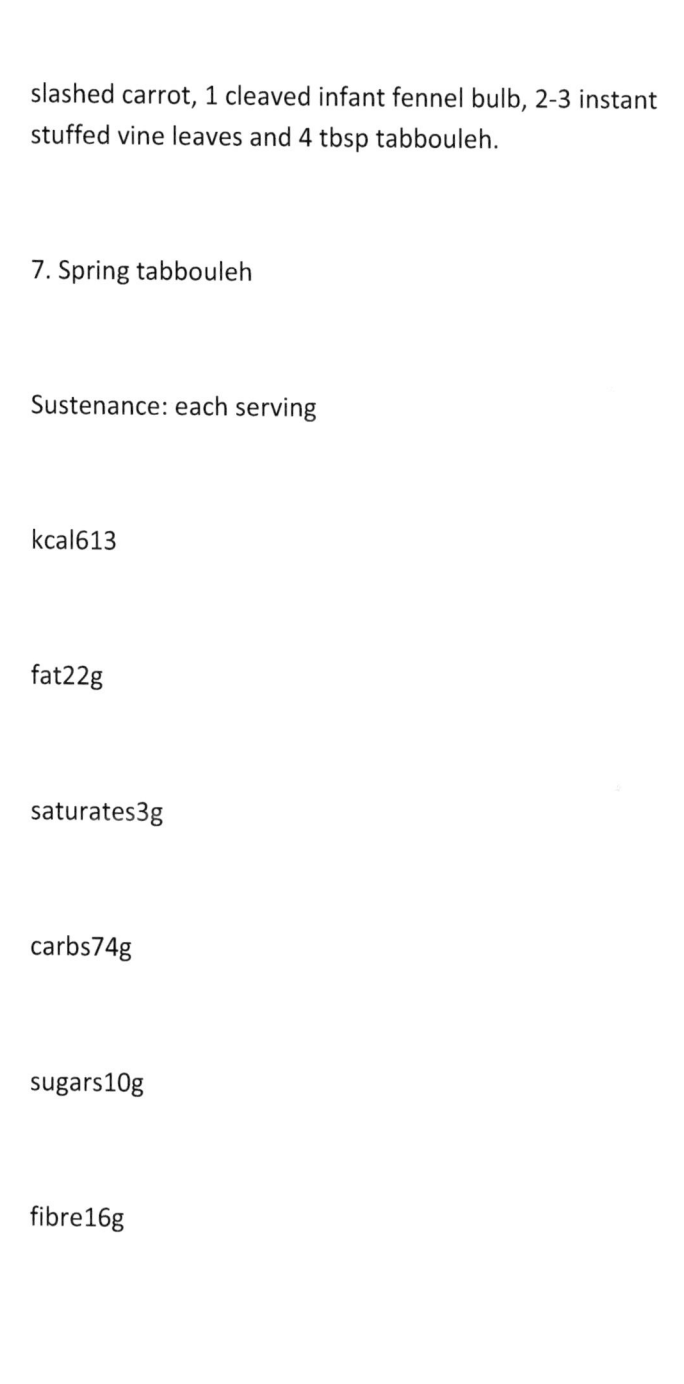

slashed carrot, 1 cleaved infant fennel bulb, 2-3 instant stuffed vine leaves and 4 tbsp tabbouleh.

7. Spring tabbouleh

Sustenance: each serving

kcal613

fat22g

saturates3g

carbs74g

sugars10g

fibre16g

protein20g

salt0g

Ingredients

6 tablespoon Olive oil

1 tablespoon garam masala

2 x 400g jars chickpeas, depleted and flushed

250g prepared to-eat blended grain pocket

250g Frozen peas

2 lemons, zested and squeezed

enormous pack parsley, leaves generally slashed

enormous pack mint, leaves generally slashed

250g Radishes, generally cut

1 Chopped

pomegranate Seeds, to work

Strategy

1. Warmth broiler to 200C/180C fan/gas . Combine 4 tablespoons oil with the garam masala and some flavoring. Hurl together with the chickpeas in an enormous broiling tin, at that point cook for 15 mins until starting to fresh. Clue in the consolidated grains, peas and lemon get-up-and-go. Blend well, at that point return to the stove for roughly 10 mins until warmed through.

2. Move into an enormous bowl or dish, at that point hurl Via the herbs, radishes, cucumber, staying oil and lemon juice. Season to taste and dissipate the pomegranate seeds. Any scraps will be useful for lunch the next day.

8. Veggie olive wraps with mustard vinaigrette

Sustenance: each serving

kcal281

fat12g

saturates2g

carbs31g

sugars12g

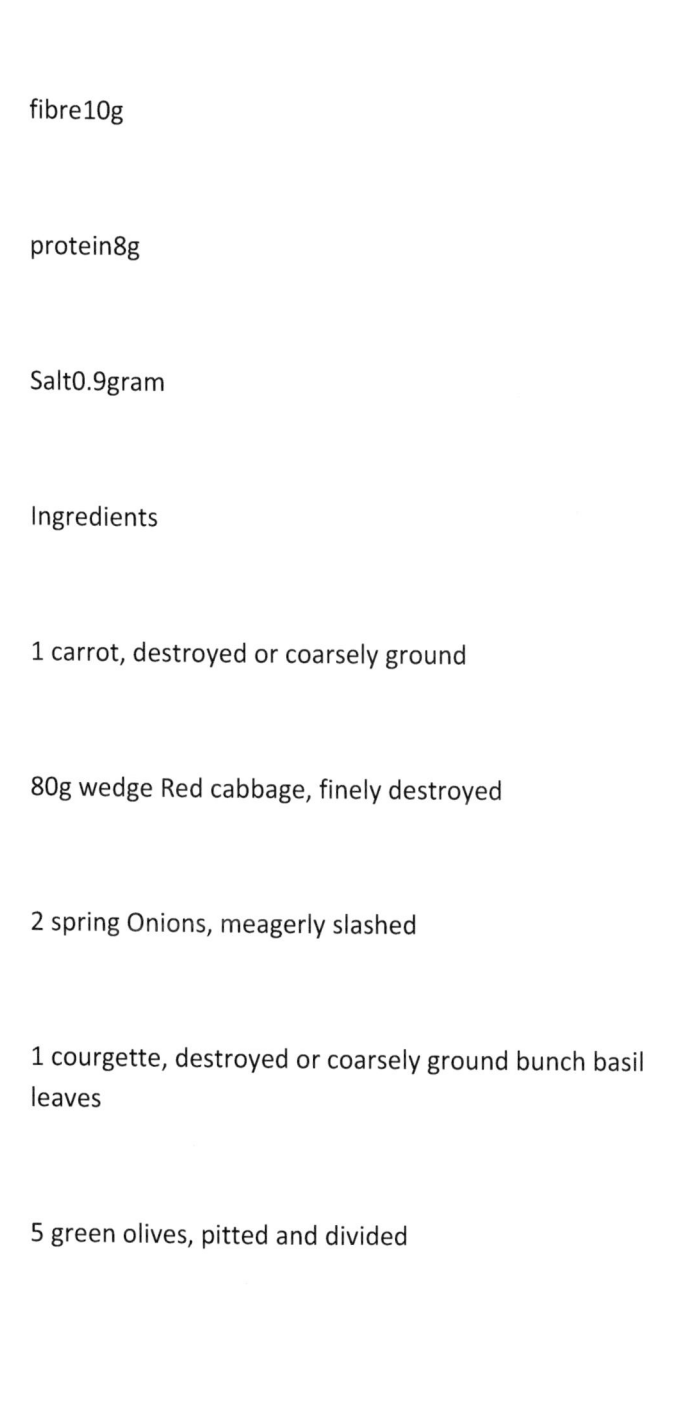

fibre10g

protein8g

Salt0.9gram

Ingredients

1 carrot, destroyed or coarsely ground

80g wedge Red cabbage, finely destroyed

2 spring Onions, meagerly slashed

1 courgette, destroyed or coarsely ground bunch basil leaves

5 green olives, pitted and divided

1/2 tsp English mustard powder

2 tsp Additional virgin rapeseed oil

1 tablespoon juice vinegar

1 major seeded tortilla

Strategy

1. Blend the entirety of the ingredients aside from the tortilla And toss well.

2. Set the tortilla onto a sheet of straightforwardness and load the Filling crosswise over one side of this wrap - it'll nearly appear to be an extreme measure of the blend, however when you start to move it safely it will be minimized. Roll the tortilla in the side, collapsing in the sides as you move. Overlay the foil at the closures to store things inside the wrapping. Cut down the middle and eat right away. In the case of taking to work, make total and wrap up simply like a wafer in preparing

material.

9. Spring tabbouleh

Nourishment: each serving

kcal613

fat22g

saturates3g

carbs74g

sugars10g

fibre16g

protein 20g

salt 0g

Ingredients

6 tablespoon Olive oil

1 tablespoon garam masala

2 x 400g jars chickpeas, depleted and washed

250g prepared to-eat blended grain pocket

250g Frozen peas

2 lemons, zested and squeezed

huge pack parsley, leaves generally cleaved

huge pack mint, leaves generally cleaved

250g Radishes, generally cut

1 Chopped

Pomegranate seeds, to work

Strategy

1. Warmth broiler to 200C/180C aficionado/gas. Combine 4 tablespoons oil with the garam masala and some flavoring. Hurl together with the chickpeas in a huge simmering tin, at that point cook for 15 mins until starting to fresh. Clue in the consolidated grains, peas and lemon pizzazz. Blend well, at that point return to the broiler for around 10 mins until warmed through.

2. Move into a huge bowl or dish, at that point hurl Via

the herbs, radishes, cucumber, staying oil and lemon juice. Season to taste and dissipate the pomegranate seeds. Any scraps will be useful for lunch the next day.

10. Guacamole and cherry plate of mixed greens with dark beans

Nourishment: Per serving

kcal341

fat15g

saturates3g

carbs33g

sugars18g

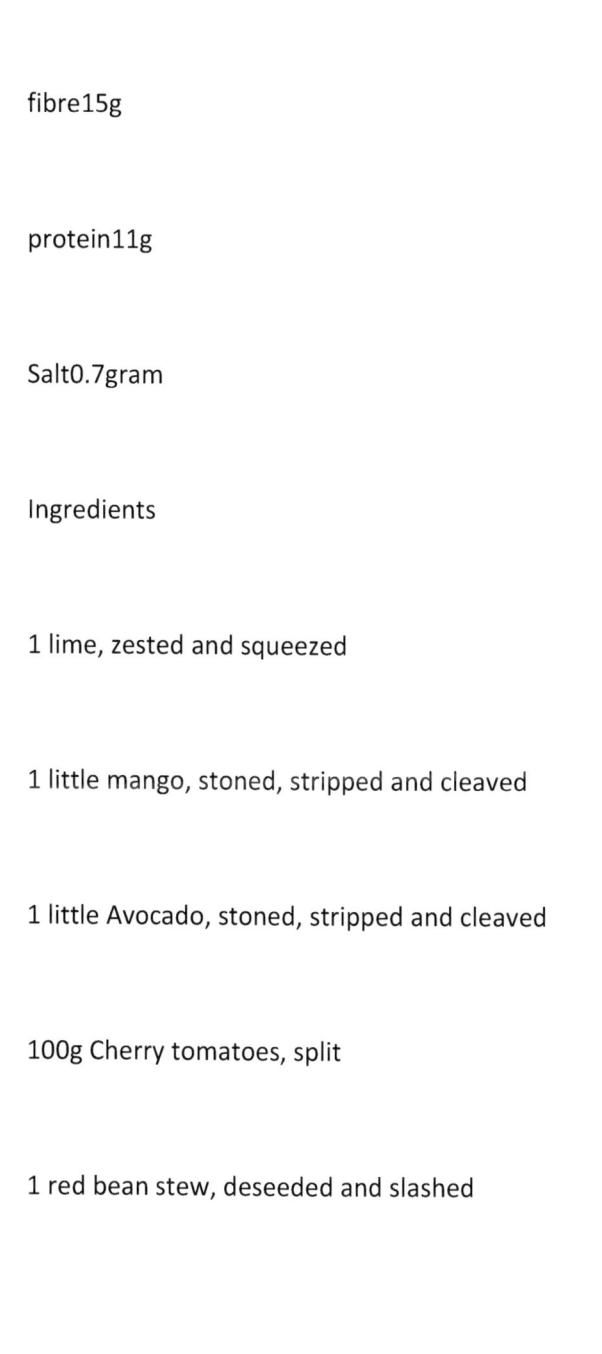

fibre 15g

protein 11g

Salt 0.7gram

Ingredients

1 lime, zested and squeezed

1 little mango, stoned, stripped and cleaved

1 little Avocado, stoned, stripped and cleaved

100g Cherry tomatoes, split

1 red bean stew, deseeded and slashed

1 red Chopped

1/2 little Pack coriander, cleaved

400g can Black beans, depleted and washed

Procedure

1. Set the lime get-up-and-go and squeeze, avocado, cherry, Tomatoes, bean stew and onion into a bowl, at that point mix through the vegetables and coriander.

11. Simple falafels

Nourishment: every falafel

kcal139

fat7g

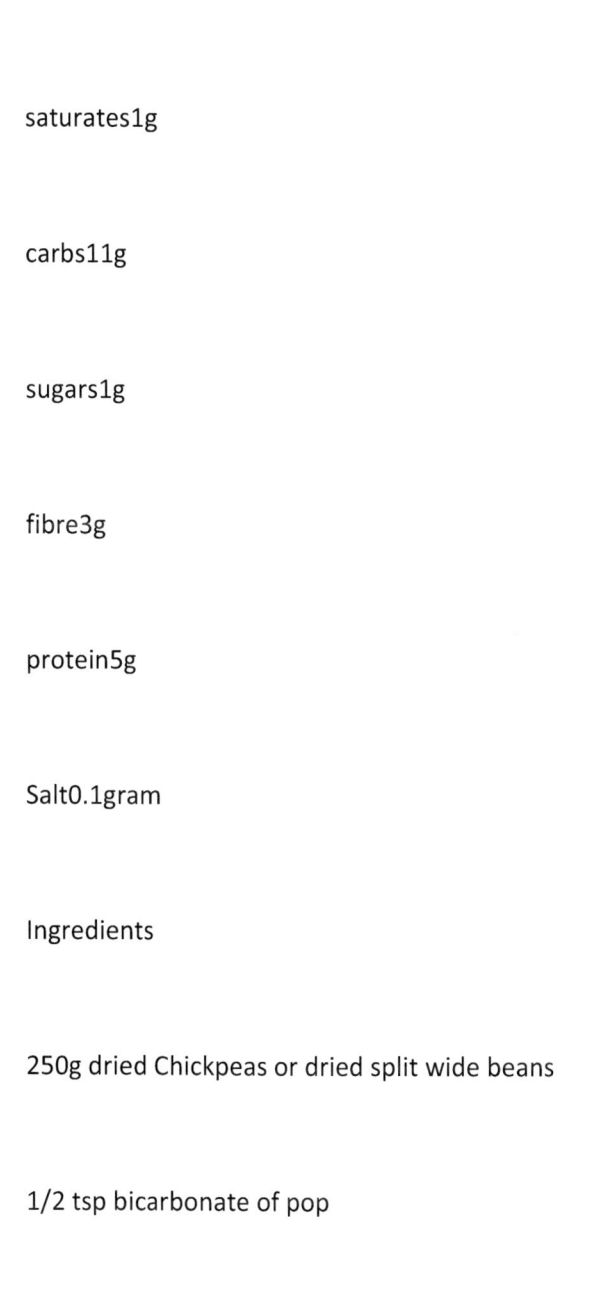

saturates 1g

carbs 11g

sugars 1g

fibre 3g

protein 5g

Salt 0.1gram

Ingredients

250g dried Chickpeas or dried split wide beans

1/2 tsp bicarbonate of pop

3 garlic cloves

1 onion, generally hacked

1 leek, generally hacked

1 celery Stick, generally cut

1 little Chili, generally cut (deseeded in the event that you loathe it too hot)

1 teaspoon ground cumin

1 teaspoon cayenne pepper

1 teaspoon sumac

Extraordinary bunch slashed coriander

Extraordinary Couple slashed parsley

80g g flour

100ml Vegetable oil

To work

houmous, Tabbouleh and salted red onion and radish (see goes pleasantly with), flatbreads, shop-purchased or see goes pleasantly with (discretionary)

Procedure

1. Absorb the chickpeas cold water for 2 hrs, or medium-term.

2. Channel the chickpeas and heartbeat utilizing the bicarb in a nourishment processor until generally

cleaved. Dispense with 3/4 of this blend and set aside.

3. Include the garlic, vegetables, herbs and flavors to The remainder of the blend in the chip and purée into a glue. Mix the glue to the extreme purée of chickpeas, include the g flour, blend and season well.

4. Warmth stove to 110C/90C fan/gas 1/4. Warmth a huge, Non-stick skillet over a moderate warmth and include a couple of this oil. Utilize your hands to frame the blend into patties (there should be adequate to make around 16). Fry for two mins each side until fresh. Keep in a warm broiler while you fry the remainder of the blend, proceeding to carry a little oil into the container with each group. Serve enclosed by flatbreads, in the event that you like, together with the houmous, tabbouleh and salted red onion and radish.

12. Quick hummus

Sustenance: each serving

kcal416

fat38g

saturates5g

carbs8g

sugars1g

fibre4g

protein8g

Salt0.1gram

13. Quick hummus

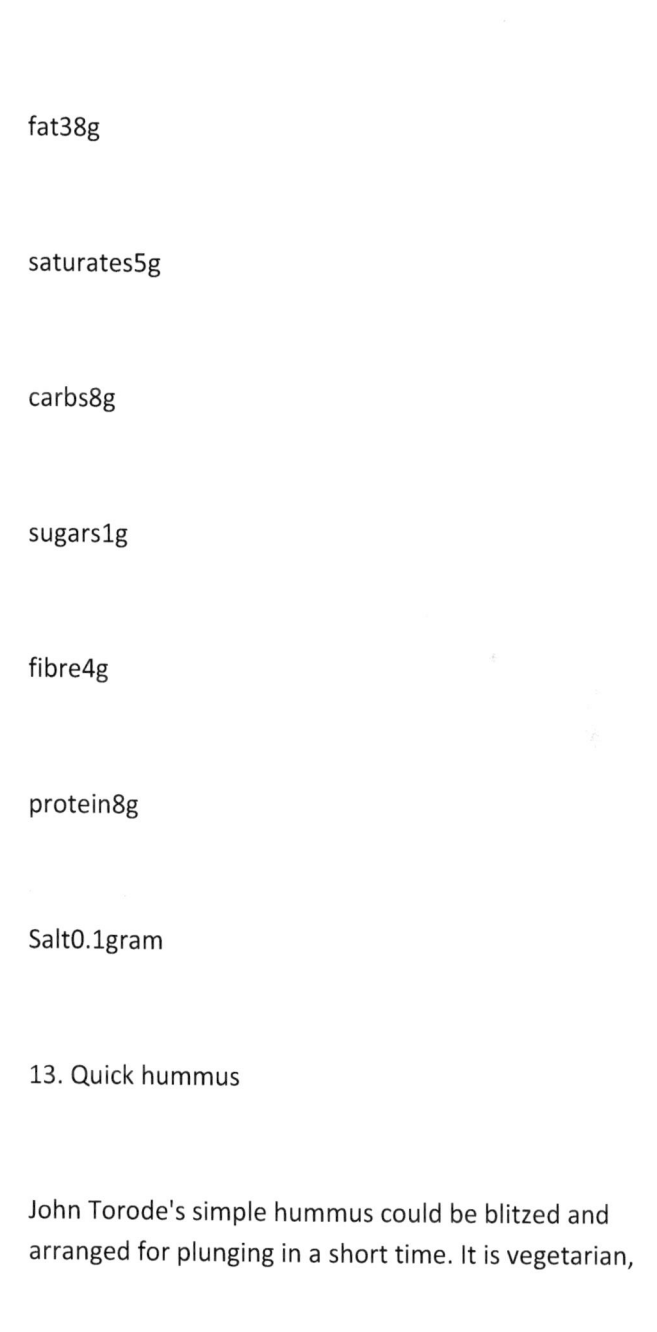

John Torode's simple hummus could be blitzed and arranged for plunging in a short time. It is vegetarian, matured and pivotal to some meze or veggie feast

Sans gluten

Veggie lover

Veggie lover

Sustenance: each serving

kcal416

fat38g

saturates5g

carbs8g

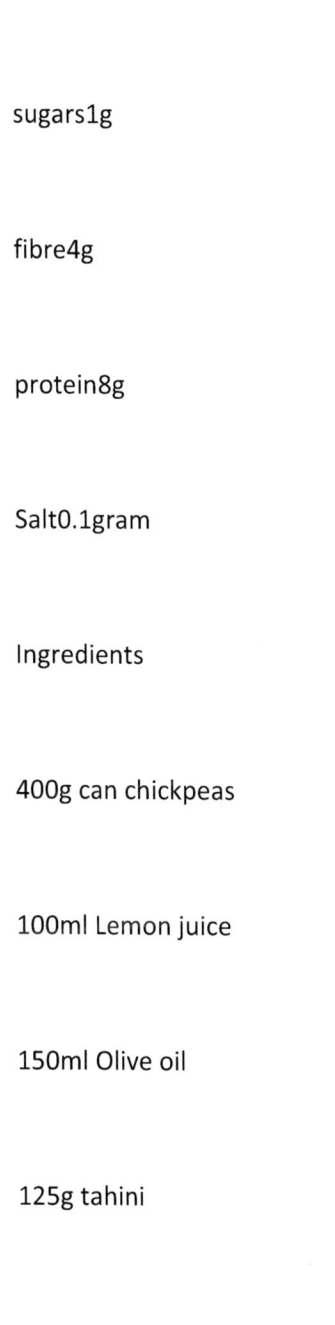

sugars 1g

fibre 4g

protein 8g

Salt 0.1gram

Ingredients

400g can chickpeas

100ml Lemon juice

150ml Olive oil

125g tahini

1/2 tsp ground coriander

5 cardamom units

toasted pine nuts

sumac

Technique

1. Channel The container of chickpeas, looking after water. Tenderly warm in a microwave, at that pointed tip into a nourishment processor with the lemon juice, olive oil, tahini, ground coriander and squashed seeds from the cardamom units. Mix till smooth - put in a scramble of chickpea water when it is looking somewhat dry. Check the flavoring and include more oil and lemon juice to taste. Serve sprinkled with toasted pine nuts and sumac.

14. Broiled cauli-Broc bowl with tahini hummus

Nourishment: each serving

kcal533

fat37g

saturates4g

carbs28g

sugars6g

fibre10g

protein16g

Salt0.8gram

Ingredients

400g bundle Steak and broccoli florets

2 tablespoon Olive oil

250g prepared to-eat quinoa

2 cooked beetroots, cut

Huge Couple infant spinach

10 pecans

, toasted and hacked

2 tablespoon tahini

3 tablespoon hummus

1 lemon, 1/2 squeezed, 1/2 cut into wedges

Technique

1. The night ahead, heat stove to 200C/180C fan/gas 6. Set the broccoli and cauliflower in an enormous skillet with all the oil and a sprinkle of flaky ocean salt. Broil for 25-30 mins until sautéed and cooked. Leave to cool totally.

2. Build each bowl by setting a large portion of the quinoa in each. Lay the bits of beetroot on top, pursued with the spinach, broccoli, cauliflower and pecans. Mix the tahini, hummus lemon juice and 1 tbsp water in a little pot. Preceding eating, coat at the dressing table. Present with the lemon wedges.

15. Crunchy bulgur serving of mixed greens

Sustenance: each serving

kcal483

fat22g

saturates2g

carbs50g

sugars11g

fibre9g

protein17g

salt0g

Ingredients

200g bulgur wheat

150g Suspended podded edamame (soya) vegetables

Two Romano peppers, cut into adjusts, seeds evacuated

150g radishes , finely slashed

75g whole whitened almonds

Little Bunch mint, finely slashed

Little bundle parsley, finely cleaved

2 oranges

3 tablespoon Extra virgin olive oil

Methodology

1. Cook the bulgur adhering to bundle guidelines, at that point Tip and channel into an enormous serving bowl to cool. In the interim, set the edamame beans in a little bowl, pour on bubbling water, leave for 1 minute, at that point channel. Put into a serving bowl with every one of the peppers, radishes, almonds, carrot, and mint.

2. Strip 1 orange, cut the areas and increment the bowl. Crush the juice of the inverse into a jam container together with the oil. Season well and shake. Pour over the plate of mixed greens, hurl well and serve

16. No-cook Festival burrito No-cook celebration burrito
Ingredients

100g bulgur wheat

120g cherry tomatoes

4 tortilla wraps

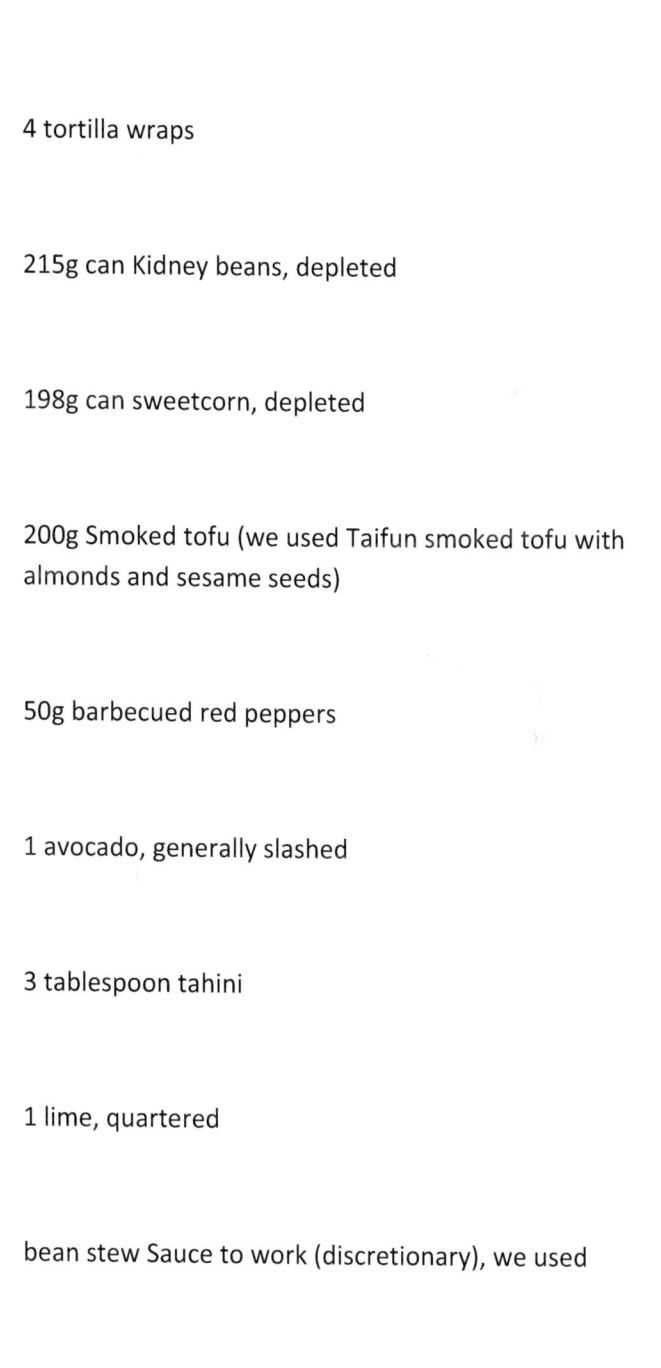

215g can Kidney beans, depleted

198g can sweetcorn, depleted

200g Smoked tofu (we used Taifun smoked tofu with almonds and sesame seeds)

50g barbecued red peppers

1 avocado, generally slashed

3 tablespoon tahini

1 lime, quartered

bean stew Sauce to work (discretionary), we used

Sriracha

You'll also need

scissors

1 moderate Food tote

outdoors plates, bowls and cutlery

a flagon of Really high temp water (min 100ml)

Methodology

1. Spot the bulgur wheat into a bowl and afterward include 100ml of bubbling water. Spread and leave to bubble for 35-40 mins.

2. Set the cherry tomatoes to a nourishment pack.

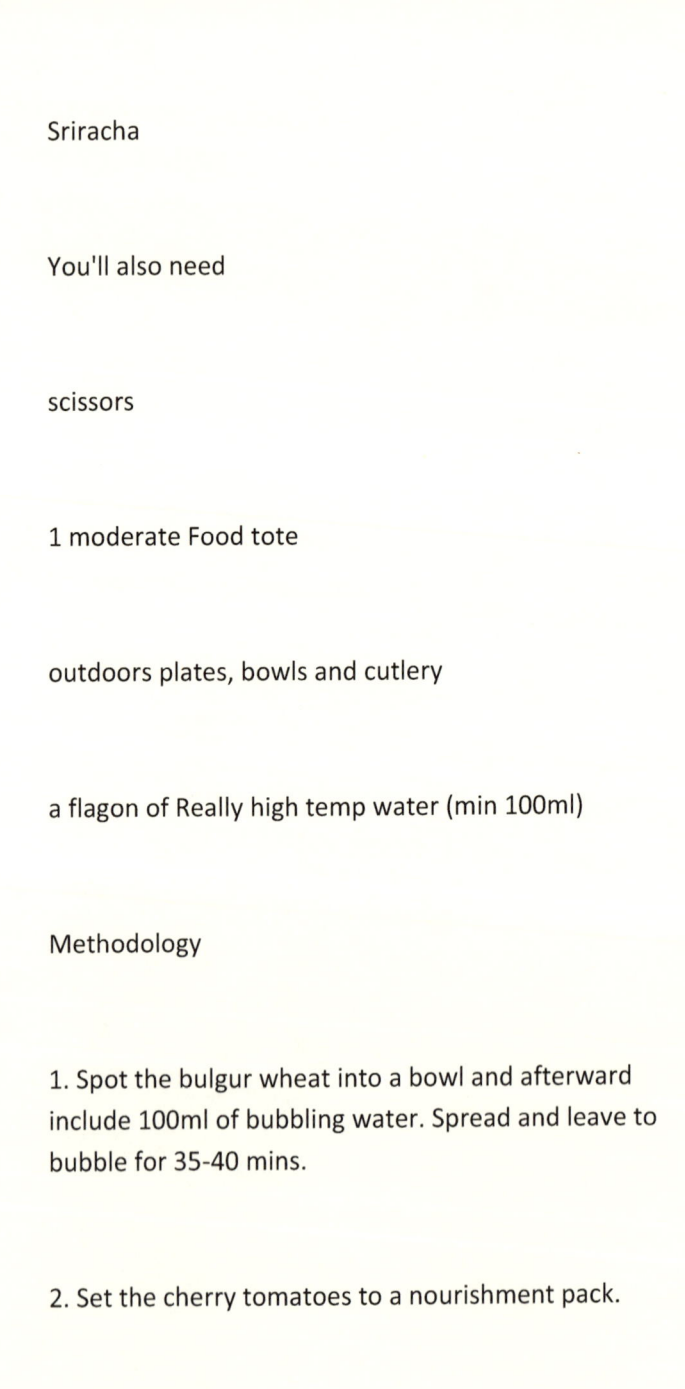

Holding The finish of the pack shut freely with a solitary had to squish the berries all through the sack with another -, for example, popping bubble wrap. This should isolate the juice in the rest of the berries without making a wreck or having a blade and cleaving load up. Delicately pour the tomato juice to the bowl of bulgur wheat, holding the tomato bits inside the pack for some other time.

3. After the bulgur wheat gets finished dousing, give It a mix and season with pepper and salt. In a little cup or bowl blend the tahini in with 3 tablespoons of water to create a smooth, pourable sauce at that point set aside.

4. Lay the tortilla wraps out on a Large board or Onto four plates and afterward split the bulgur wheat, kidney beans and sweetcorn including them (attempt to keep the filling in the inside). Disintegrate the hacked tofu on the top at that point include the cleaved tomatoes, flame-broiled peppers, avocado bits and a fabulous sprinkle of this tahini sauce, a press of lime and some skillet, in the event that you like.

5. Overlap the left and right sides of the wrapping into The middle starting and afterward roll the floor right over to completely encase the filling inside each wrap,

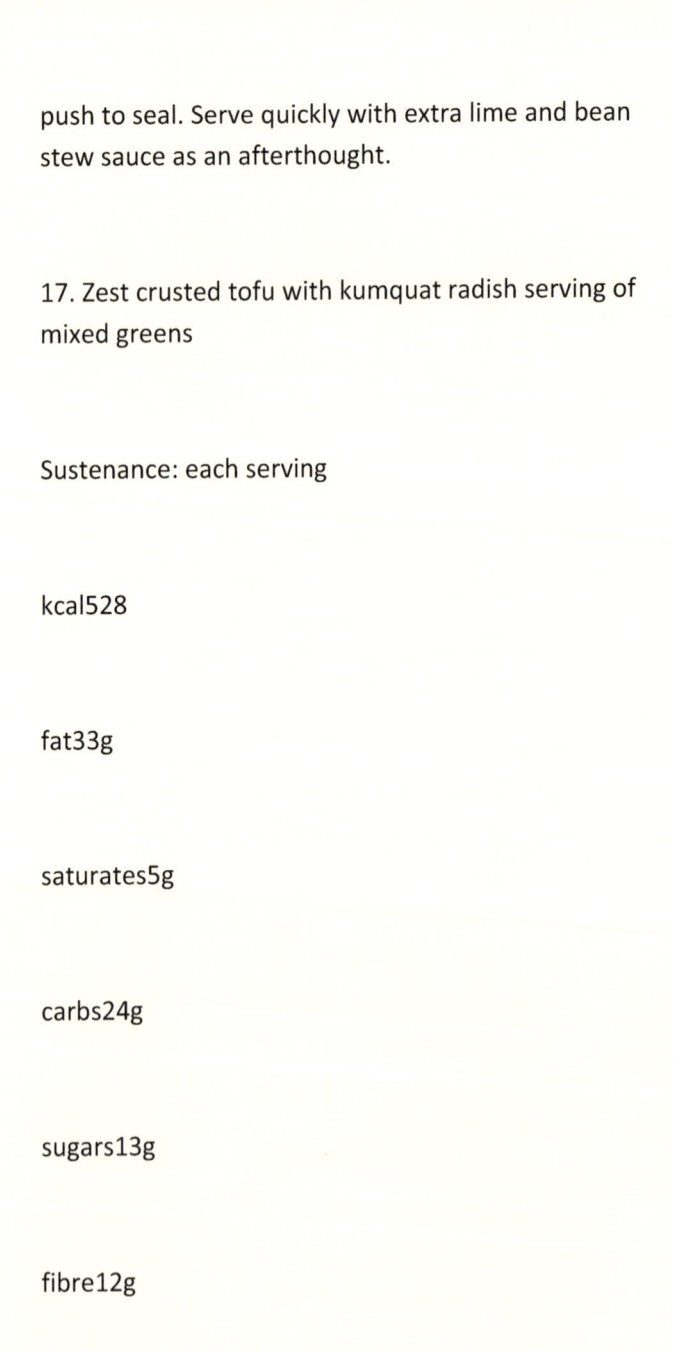

push to seal. Serve quickly with extra lime and bean stew sauce as an afterthought.

17. Zest crusted tofu with kumquat radish serving of mixed greens

Sustenance: each serving

kcal528

fat33g

saturates5g

carbs24g

sugars13g

fibre12g

protein27g

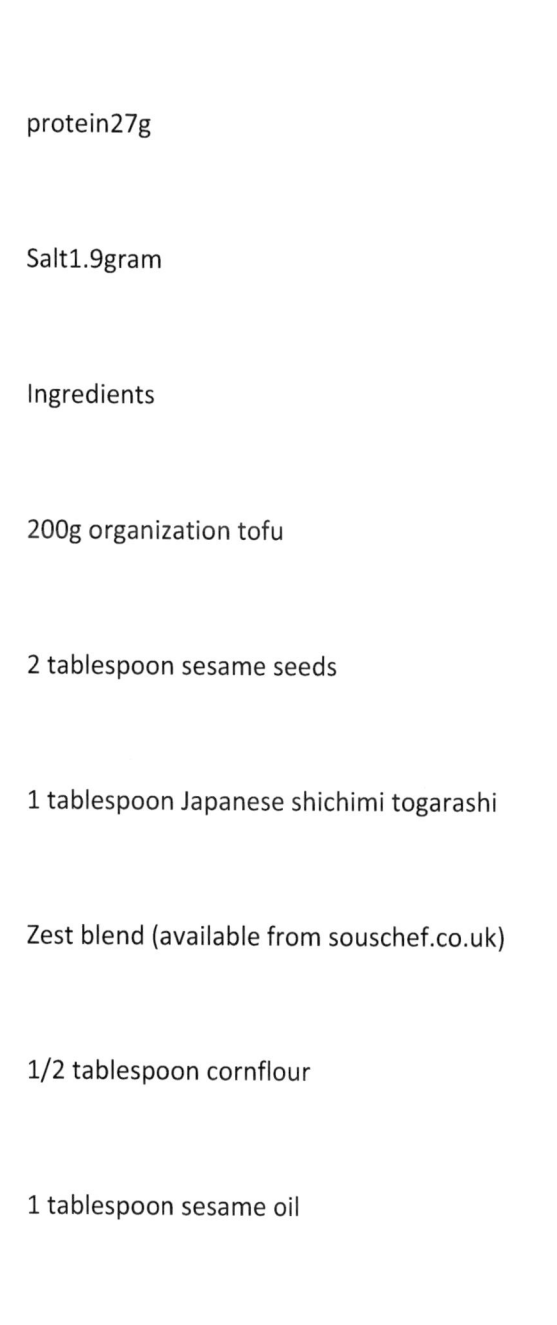

Salt1.9gram

Ingredients

200g organization tofu

2 tablespoon sesame seeds

1 tablespoon Japanese shichimi togarashi

Zest blend (available from souschef.co.uk)

1/2 tablespoon cornflour

1 tablespoon sesame oil

1 tablespoon Vegetable oil

200g Tenderstem broccoli

100g sugar snap peas

4 radishes, thinly cut

2 spring onions, finely cleaved

3 kumquats, thinly cut

For the dressing

2 tablespoon Low-salt soy sauce

2 tablespoon Yuzu juice (or 1 tablespoon each lime and lemon juice)

1 teaspoon Gold caster sugar

1 little shallot, finely diced

1 teaspoon ground ginger

Procedure

1. Cut the tofu down the middle, wrap pleasantly in kitchen Paper and spot onto a plate. Put a thick skillet on the best to press the water from it. Change the paper a few times before the tofu feels delicate, at that point cut into stout pieces. Combine the sesame seeds, Japanese zest mix, and cornflour in a bowl. Sprinkle over the tofu until all around covered. Set aside.

2. In a little bowl, consolidate the dressing ingredients together and set aside. Carry a dish of water to the bubble for the veggies and warmth the 2 oils in an enormous skillet.

3. On the off chance that the skillet Is Quite hot, include the tofu and Fry for 1 moment or so on the two sides until very much sautéed. Rehash till you've finished every one of them.

4. After the water is bubbling, cook the broccoli and Sugar snap peas for 2-3 mins. Channel and split between 2 enormous shallow dishes. Top with all the tofu and shower over the dressing table. Disperse the radishes, spring onions and kumquats on top.

18. Veggie tahini lentils

Nourishment: each serving

kcal293

fat14g

saturates2g

carbs23g

sugars7g

fibre10g

protein13g

Salt0.7gram

Ingredients

50g tahini

pizzazz and Juice 1 lemon

2 tablespoon Olive oil

1 red Onion, meagerly slashed

1 garlic clove, squashed

1 yellow Pepp

19. Dark Bean, avocado and kale rice bowl

Sustenance: each serving

kcal546

fat25g

saturates4g

carbs48g

sugars 4g

fibre 14g

protein 25g

Salt 0.8gram

Dark bean, avocado, and kale rice bowl

Serves 4

Blend your midweek suppers for this vegan Mexican dark colored rice and flame-broiled tofu supper - swap for pieces of chorizo to make it substantial

Sans gluten

Vegan

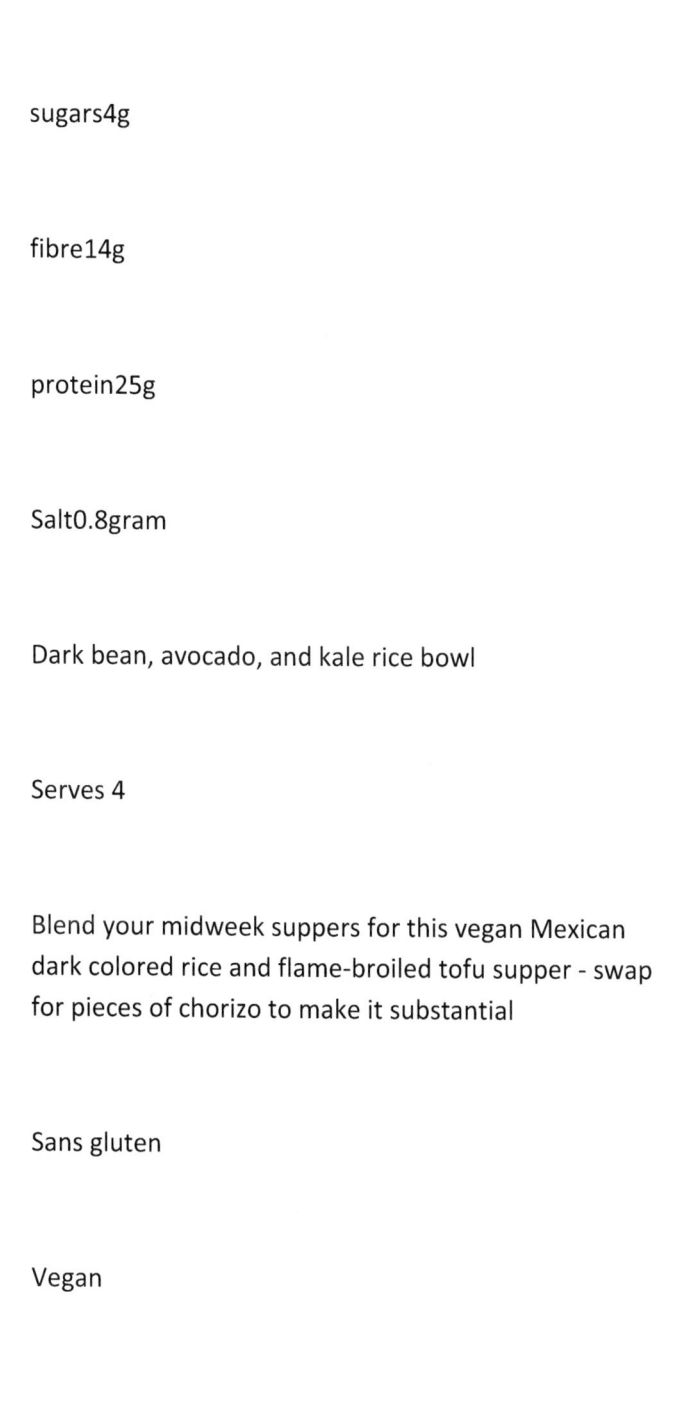

Vegetarian

Sustenance: each serving

kcal546

fat25g

saturates4g

carbs48g

sugars4g

fibre14g

protein25g

Salt 0.8gram

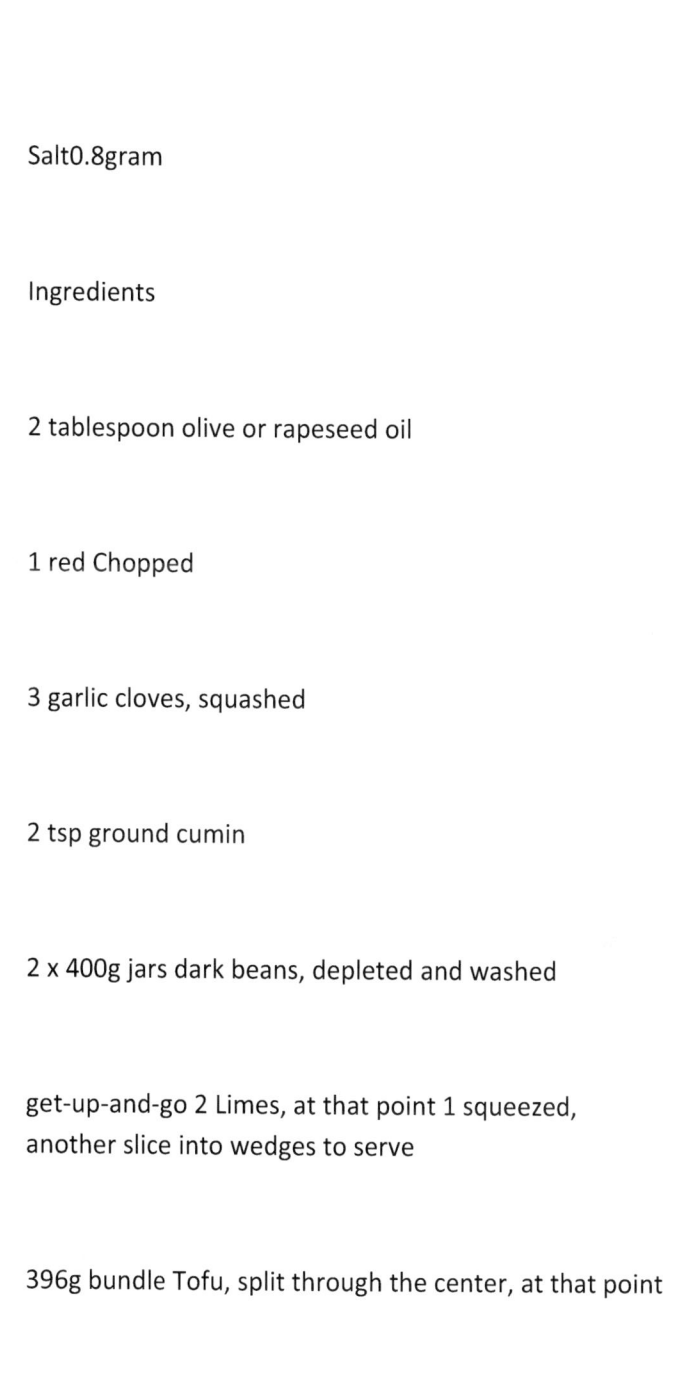

Ingredients

2 tablespoon olive or rapeseed oil

1 red Chopped

3 garlic cloves, squashed

2 tsp ground cumin

2 x 400g jars dark beans, depleted and washed

get-up-and-go 2 Limes, at that point 1 squeezed, another slice into wedges to serve

396g bundle Tofu, split through the center, at that point

cleaved into little lumps

2 tsp smoked paprika

2 x 200g pockets cooked dark colored rice

2 minimal Ripe avocados, split, stoned, stripped and cleaved

Little Bunch coriander, leaves just

1 red stew, daintily cut (discretionary)

Technique

1. Warmth the flame broil to High. Warmth 1 tablespoon oil in a Frying container, at that point, including the onion and cook, blending, for 5 mins or so until delicate. Include the garlic and stew for 30 secs longer, at that point mix in the cumin and dark beans. Cook for 5 mins before the beans start to pop and in

this manner are hot through. Mix all through the lime pizzazz and squeeze and season.

2. While the beans cook, put the tofu into a bowl and gently toss through the remainder of the oil, the paprika, and some flavoring. Line a heating plate with thwart and arrange the carrot on top. Cook under the flame broils for 5 mins each side until roasted everywhere.

3. Warmth the rice after bundle directions, at that point Split between bowls. Top with every one of the vegetables, avocado, broccoli, coriander and a wedge of lime. Include a couple of bits of stew Additionally, on the off chance that you need it hot.

20. Butternut soup with fresh sage and apple bread garnishes

Sustenance: each serving

kcal231

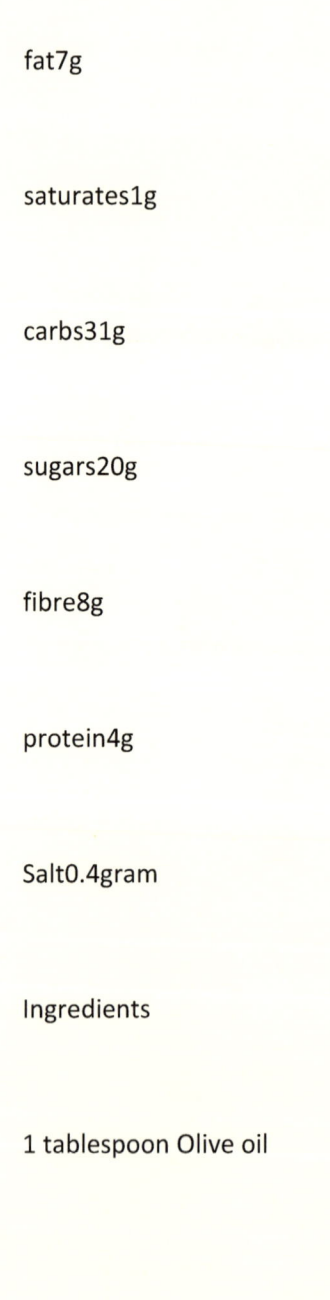

fat7g

saturates1g

carbs31g

sugars20g

fibre8g

protein4g

Salt0.4gram

Ingredients

1 tablespoon Olive oil

1 major Chopped

1 garlic clove, cut

1 Butternut squash, about 1kg, stripped, deseeded and cut

3 tablespoon Madeira or dry Sherry

500ml Fermented vegetable stock, and a little extra if necessary

1 teaspoon Chopped sage, likewise 20 little leaves, dried and cleaned

Jojoba oil, for browning

For your apple bread garnishes

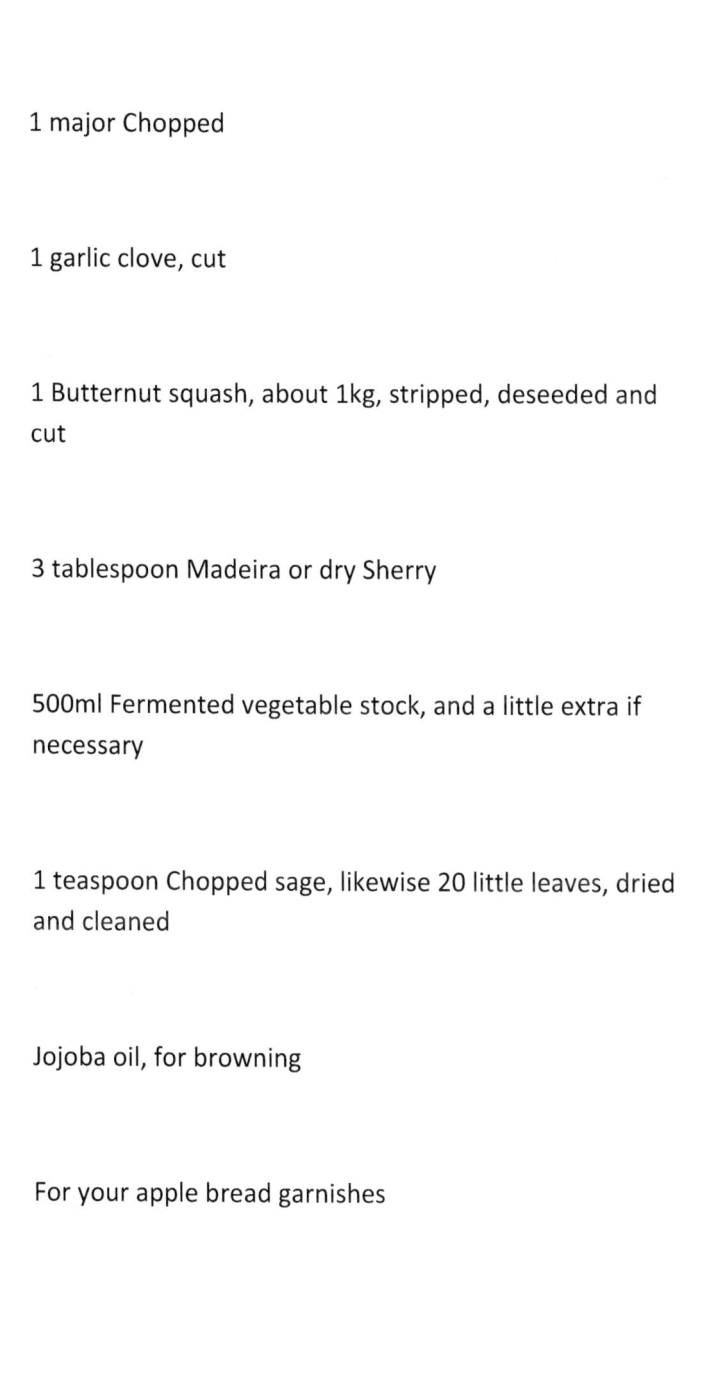

1 tablespoon Olive oil

1 major Eating apple, stripped, cored and diced

a couple of Pinches of gold caster sugar

Technique

1. Warmth the oil in a huge container, at that point include the onion and fry for 5 mins. Include the garlic and skillet, and cook for 5 mins more. Pour at the Madeira and stock, mix in the hacked rosemary, at that point spread and stew for 20 mins before the squash is delicate.

2. Rush utilizing a hand blender or in a nourishment processor until totally smooth. Permit to cool in the container, at that point cool until prepared to serve. Will keep for two days or freeze for 3 weeks. To make the firm bloom, heat some oil (a thickness of around 2cm) at a little skillet, at that point plunge from the savvy leaves till they're fresh - you'll need to do this in bunches. Channel on kitchen paper. I will keep it for a

long time.

3. Prior to serving, warm the soup in a skillet. The vibe ought to be fairly thick and smooth, however, slim it with a little stock if it's excessively thick.

4. For your apple bread garnishes, heat the oil in a huge Pan, include the carrot and apple until starting to mollify. Sprinkle with the sugar and sautéed food till softly caramelized.

1. To serve, spoon the soup into little bowls and top with the apple, savvy and a pounding of dark pepper.

21. Avocado Panzanella

Nourishment: each serving

kcal332

fat21g

saturates 4g

carbs 30g

sugars 8g

fibre 6g

protein 7g

Salt 0.9gram

Ingredients

800g blend Of ready tomatoes

1 garlic clove, squashed

11/2 tablespoon tricks, depleted and flushed

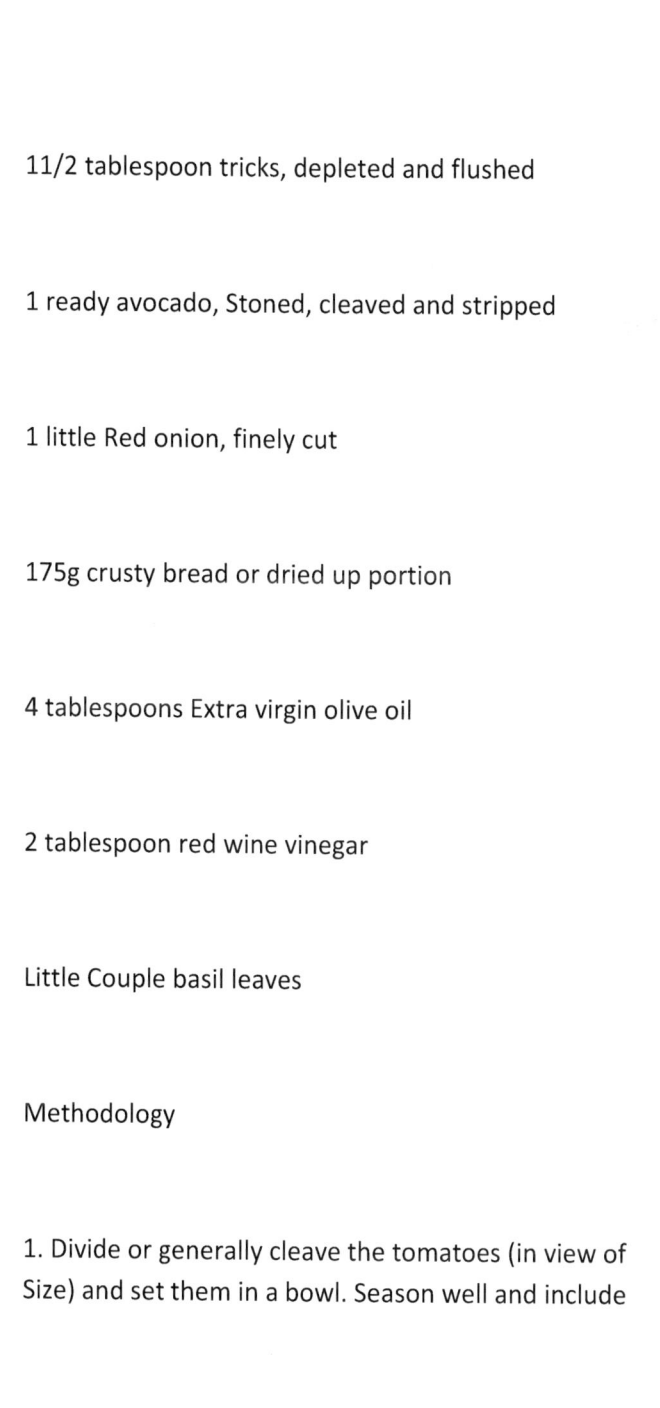

1 ready avocado, Stoned, cleaved and stripped

1 little Red onion, finely cut

175g crusty bread or dried up portion

4 tablespoons Extra virgin olive oil

2 tablespoon red wine vinegar

Little Couple basil leaves

Methodology

1. Divide or generally cleave the tomatoes (in view of Size) and set them in a bowl. Season well and include

the garlic, escapades, avocado, and onion, and blend well. Set aside for 10 mins.

2. Then, cut or tear the crusty bread into 3cm Chunks and put in a huge serving bowl or on a platter. Sprinkle with half of the olive oil, half of the vinegar and afterward include a spoonful. At the point when prepared to serve, pour over the berries and some different juices. Disperse with the basil leaves and sprinkle over the rest of the vinegar and oil. Give it a last mix and serve right away.

22. Bulgur and wide bean serving of mixed greens with a lively dressing

Nourishment: each serving

kcal443

fat13g

saturates2g

carbs62g

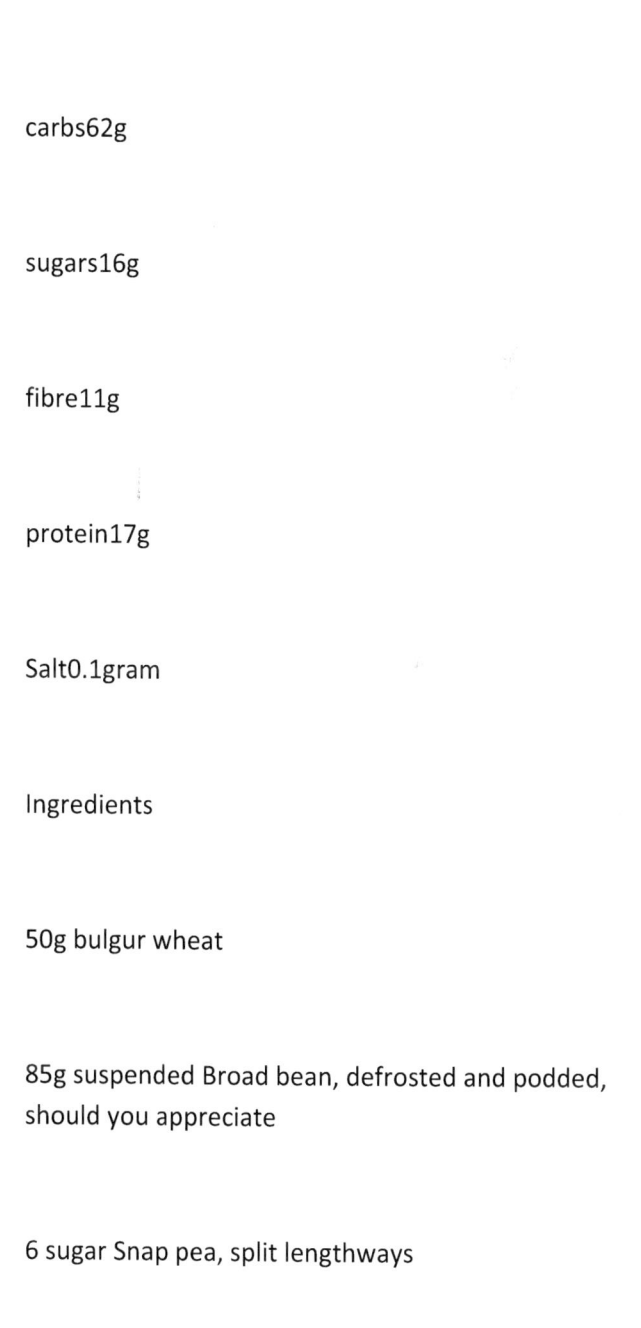

sugars16g

fibre11g

protein17g

Salt0.1gram

Ingredients

50g bulgur wheat

85g suspended Broad bean, defrosted and podded, should you appreciate

6 sugar Snap pea, split lengthways

4 radish

, daintily cut

1/2 minimal Red onion, daintily hacked

Little Couple mint

Leaves

For the dressing

get-up-and-go and Coffee 1 lime

1/2 minimal red stew, deseeded and cleaved

1 tablespoon extra-virgin olive oil

1 teaspoon White wine vinegar

1 teaspoon clear nectar

Procedure

1. Cook the bulgur wheat after pack Instructions, including the wide beans to the last 2 mins. Cool under chilly running water, at that point channel well, at that point hurl with the sugar snap peas, radishes, and red onion.

2. Whisk together the dressing ingredients together with a couple of Seasoning and prepare all through the serving of mixed greens. Dissipate with the mint leaves.

23. Herby Celery and bulgur serving of mixed greens

Sustenance: each serving

kcal229

fat10g

saturates1g

carbs30g

sugars5g

fibre2g

protein4g

Salt0.1gram

Ingredients

200g bulgur wheat

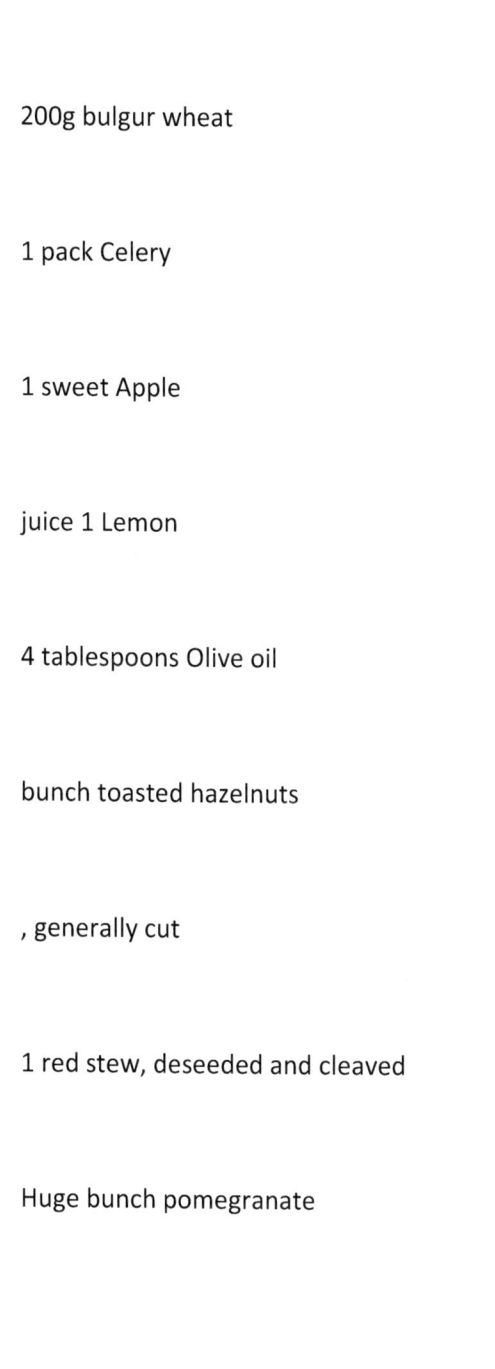

1 pack Celery

1 sweet Apple

juice 1 Lemon

4 tablespoons Olive oil

bunch toasted hazelnuts

, generally cut

1 red stew, deseeded and cleaved

Huge bunch pomegranate

Seeds

Little pack parsley

, slashed

Little Cluster mint

, slashed

Little bundle tarragon

, slashed

Methodology

1. Spot the bulgur wheat in an enormous bowl and afterward just spread with bubbling water. Spread the bowl with stick film and leave for 30 mins to devour the

entirety of the water.

2. In the interim, separate the sticks of celery and furthermore place The leaves separated. Finely cut the celery and generally slash the leaves. Cut the apple into fine matchsticks and hurl in a little lemon juice. In a bowl blend the rest of the lemon squeeze in with the oil alongside some flavoring to make a dressing table.

3. Delicately cushion up the bulgur with a fork. Blend the Chopped apple and celery all through the bulgur, pursued with the nuts, stew, pomegranate seeds, and herbs. Sprinkle over the dressing and hurl everything together delicately. Dissipate with the celery leaves and capacity.

24. Curried squash, lentil, and coconut soup

Sustenance: each serving

kcal178

fat7g

saturates5g

carbs22g

sugars9g

fibre4g

protein6g

Salt0.4gram

Ingredients

1 tablespoon Olive oil

1 butternut squash, stripped, deseeded and diced

200g carrot

, diced

1 tablespoon Curry powder including turmeric

100g red lentil

700ml low-sodium vegetable stock

1 may diminished fat coconut milk

coriander And naan bread, to work

Strategy

1. Warmth the oil in an enormous pot, include the skillet And carrots, sizzle for 1 minute, at that point mix in the curry powder and cook 1 minute more. The indication from the peas, the vegetable stock, and coconut milk and give everything a decent mix. Bring to the bubble, at that point turn down the warmth and stew for 15-18 mins until all are delicate.

2. With a hand blender or in a nourishment processor, Blitz until as simple as you'd like. Season and serve sprinkled with generally cleaved coriander and some naan bread together with.

25. Moroccan spiced Steak and vanilla soup

Sustenance: each serving

kcal200

fat16g

saturates2g

carbs8g

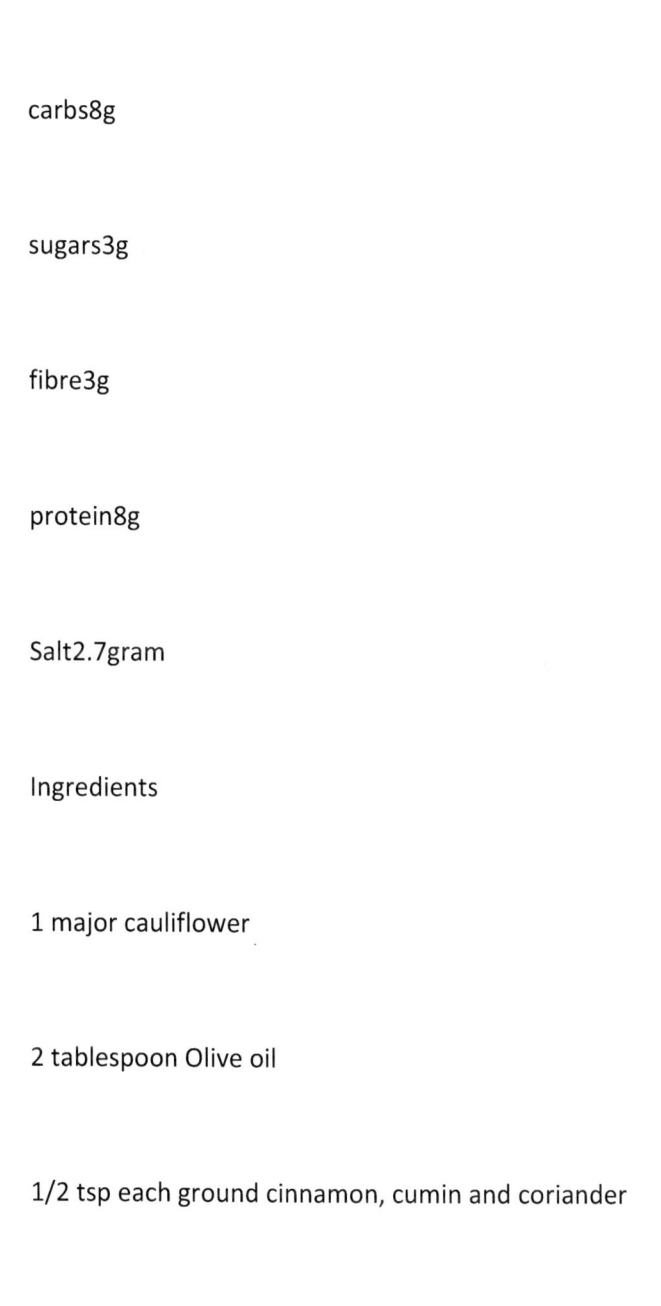

sugars3g

fibre3g

protein8g

Salt2.7gram

Ingredients

1 major cauliflower

2 tablespoon Olive oil

1/2 tsp each ground cinnamon, cumin and coriander

2 tablespoon Harissa glue, and an additional sprinkle

1l attractive Vegetable or chicken stock

50g Toasted chipped almond, and extra to serve

Technique

Cut the cauliflower into little florets. Fry olive Petroleum, ground cinnamon, cumin and coriander and harissa glue for 2 mins at a major dish. Include the cauliflower, stock, and almonds. Spread and cook for 20 mins before the cauliflower is delicate. Mix soup until smooth, at that point work with an abundance shower of harissa and a sprinkle of toasted almonds.

CHAPTER SIX

Dinner Recipes

Veggie lover bean stew

Serves 4

This dish proliferates packs in a lot of vegetables and doesn't miss the mark on the flavor. Serve it with rice coat potatoes for a filling dinner

Sustenance: Per serving

kcal367

fat10g

saturates2g

carbs48g

sugars22g

fibre17g

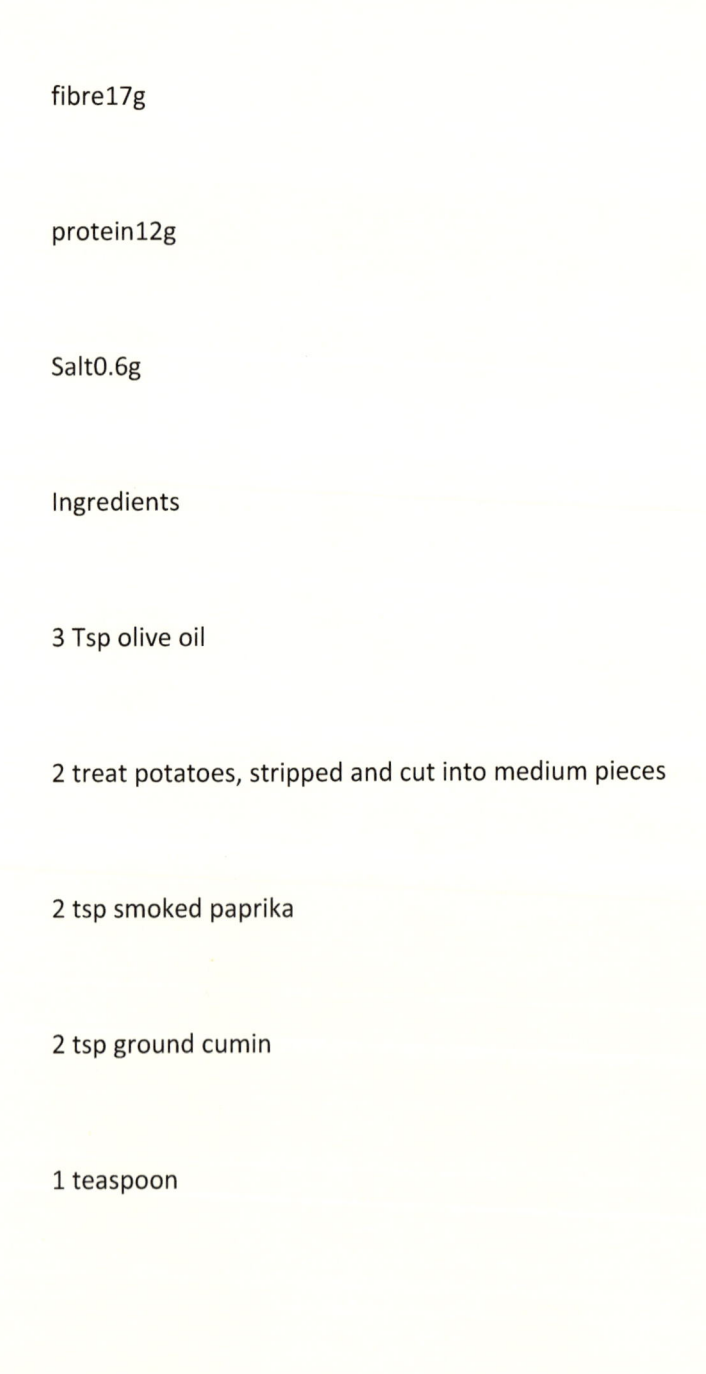

protein12g

Salt0.6g

Ingredients

3 Tsp olive oil

2 treat potatoes, stripped and cut into medium pieces

2 tsp smoked paprika

2 tsp ground cumin

1 teaspoon

, cleaved

2 Carrots stripped and cleaved

2 celery Sticks, cleaved

2 garlic cloves, squashed

1-2 tsp bean stew powder (contingent upon how hot you like it)

1 tsp dried oregano

1 Tbsp tomato purée

1 red pepper, cut into lumps

2 x 400g jars cleaved tomatoes

400g can Black beans, depleted

400g may Kidney beans, depleted

Lime Wedges, guacamole, wheat and rice to work

Strategy

1. Warming Oven to 200C/180C fan/gas 6. Set up the Sweet potato pieces into a broiling tin and shower more than 11/2 tsp oil, 1 tsp smoked paprika and 1 tsp ground cumin. Give everything a fantastic blend so the balls have been covered in flavors, season with salt and pepper at that point broil for 25 mins until cooked.

2. In the meantime, heat the oil in an enormous pot over medium warmth. Include the onion, carrot, and celery. Cook for 8-10 mins, blending infrequently until delicate at that point pound the garlic and cook for 1 minute longer. Include the rest of the flavors and tomato puree. Give everything a fantastic blend and cook for a brief length.

3. Include The red pepper, cleaved tomatoes, and 200ml Of water. Heat the bean stew to the point of boiling at that point stew for 20 mins. Tip from the beans and cook for another 10 mins before coordinating the sweet potato. Season to taste at that point present with lime wedges, guac, rice, and coriander. Make in advance and freeze as long as 3 months.

To make this in a toaster:

Warmth the oil in a skillet on a medium Warmth. Include the onion, carrot and celery. Cook for 8-10 mins, blending at times until delicate at that point pound the garlic, at that point stunt from the sweet potato lumps and cook for 1 minute longer. Include every one of the flavors which are dried, dried and tomato puree, cook for a moment at that point stunt the entire parcel into a toaster.

Include the red pepper and cleaved tomatoes. Give Everything a decent mix at that point cook on low for 5 hrs. Mix in the beans and cook for an additional 30 mins to 1 hr. Season to taste and present with lime wedges, guac, rice and coriander.

Veggie lover chickpea Curry coat potatoes

Nourishment: Per serving

kcal276

fat9g

saturates3g

carbs32g

sugars12g

fibre11g

protein12g

Salt 0.3g

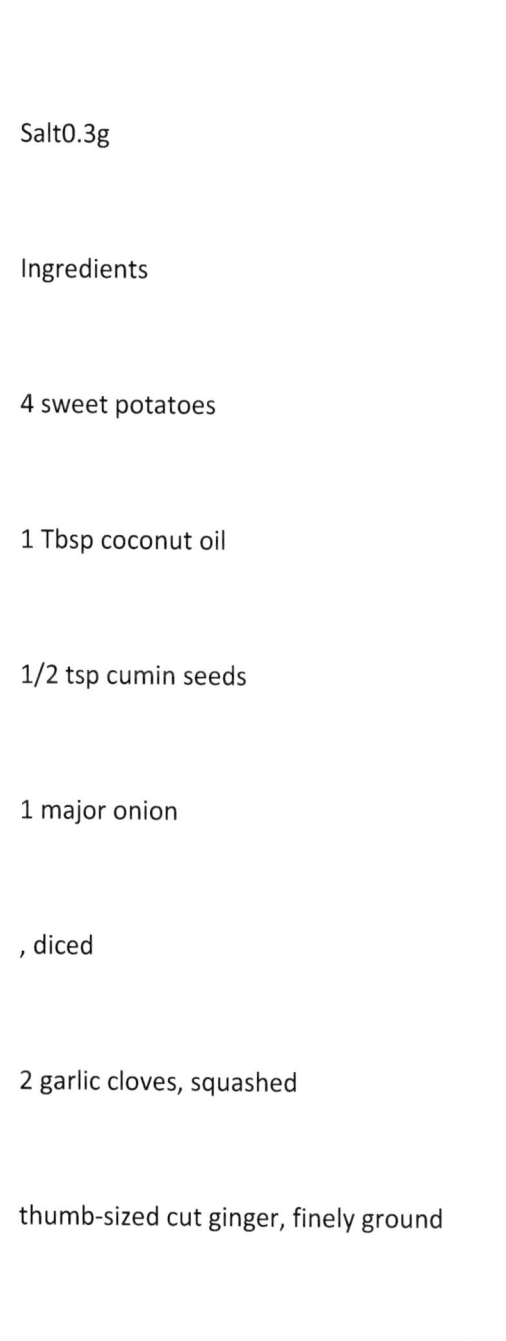

Ingredients

4 sweet potatoes

1 Tbsp coconut oil

1/2 tsp cumin seeds

1 major onion, diced

2 garlic cloves, squashed

thumb-sized cut ginger, finely ground

1 green bean stew, finely cleaved

1 tsp garam masala

1 tsp ground coriander

1/2 tsp turmeric

2 Tbsp tikka masala glue

2 x 400g can cleaved tomatoes

2 x 400g can chickpeas, depleted

Lemon

Wedges and coriander leaves, to work

Plan

1. Warming Oven to 200C/180C fan/gas 6. Prick the Sweet potatoes around with a fork, at that point put onto a heating plate and meal in the broiler for 45 mins or until delicate when penetrated with a blade.

2. In the interim, Melt the coconut oil in a huge Saucepan over medium warmth. Include the cumin seeds and fry for 1 moment until fragrant, at that point, including the onion and stew for 7-10 mins until mollified.

3. Set the ginger, garlic and green bean stew into the container, and cook for 2-3 mins. Include the flavors and tikka masala glue and cook for a further 2 mins until sweet-smelling, at that pointed tip into the berries. Bring to a stew, at that pointed tip from the chickpeas and cook for a further 20 mins until thickened. Season.

4. Spot The simmered sweet potatoes on four plates at that point cut lengthways. Spoon inside the chickpea curry at that point crush the lemon wedges. Season, at

that point dissipate coriander before serving.

Veggie lover hotdog rolls

Nourishment: Per serving

kcal326

fat20g

saturates8g

carbs27g

sugars3g

fibre4g

protein 7g

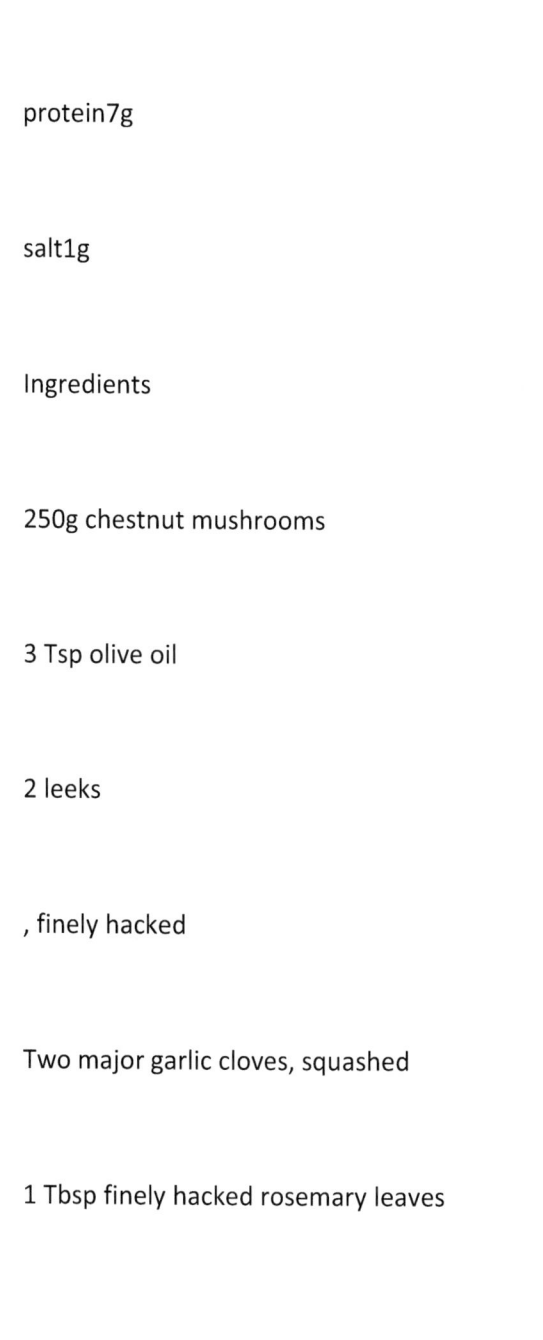

salt 1g

Ingredients

250g chestnut mushrooms

3 Tsp olive oil

2 leeks, finely hacked

Two major garlic cloves, squashed

1 Tbsp finely hacked rosemary leaves

1 Tbsp dark colored rice miso

2 tsp Dijon mustard

30g chestnuts, finely hacked

70g new white breadcrumbs

1 x 320g Sheet prepared moved puff cake (not the all-spread variation)

plain flour for tidying

sans dairy milk

(like soya milk), to coat

Plan

1. Tip the mushrooms into a nourishment processor and heartbeat until they are finely cleaved. Put a large portion of the olive oil in a skillet, include the leeks alongside a touch of salt and stew for 15 mins or until mollified and brilliant darker. Scratch the leeks in the panto a bowl and put aside to cool fairly.

2. Warmth the Remainder of the oil in the dish and fry the mushrooms for 10 mins over medium warmth. Include the garlic, sage, miso and mustard, and stew for a further moment. Leave to cool to some degree.

3. Warmth The toaster into 200C/180C fan/gas 6. A proposal the Mushroom blend into the bowl with the leeks, at that point, include the chestnuts and breadcrumbs. Season, at that point consolidate everything together until you have acquired a marginally hardened blend.

4. Unwind The cake on a floured surface, at that point Roll the baked good out to ensure a solitary side estimates 43 cm. Form the mushroom and leek blend into a wiener shape down the focal point of the baked good, at that point put the cake up around the filling and curve all through the crease utilizing a fork. Cut into ten pieces. Lay a material lined preparing sheet and

brush each piece with milk. Prepare for 25 mins or until profound, brilliant dark-colored. Leave to cool a tad and sprinkle with sesame seeds before serving.

Veggie lover brownies

Sustenance: Per serving

kcal314

fat16g

saturates6g

carbs36g

sugars25g

fibre3g

protein5g

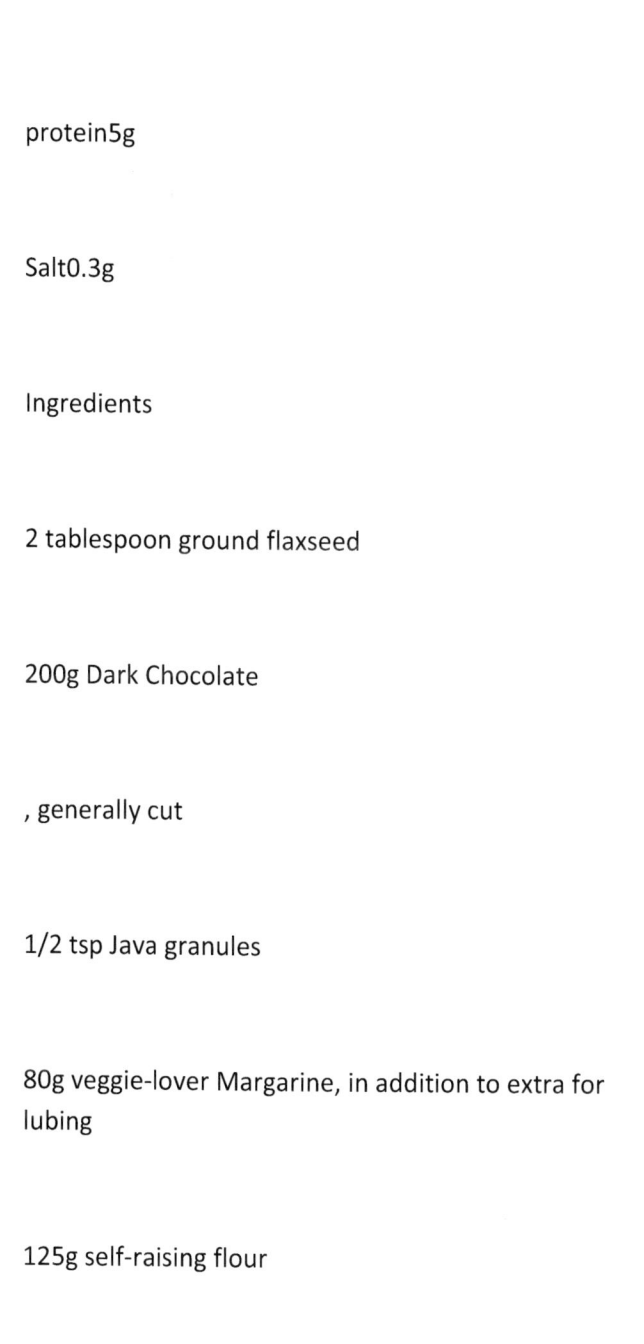

Salt0.3g

Ingredients

2 tablespoon ground flaxseed

200g Dark Chocolate

, generally cut

1/2 tsp Java granules

80g veggie-lover Margarine, in addition to extra for lubing

125g self-raising flour

70g ground surface peppers

50g cocoa powder

1/4 tsp heating powder

250g Gold caster sugar

11/2 tsp vanilla concentrate

Technique

1. Warming Oven to 170C/150C fan/gas 31/2. Oil and line a 20cm square tin with preparing material. Consolidate the yolk with 6 tbsp water and put in a safe spot for at any rate 5 mins.

2. In A pot, liquefy 120g chocolate, the espresso, and Margarine with 60ml water on truly low warmth. Permit

to cool marginally.

3. Set the bread, avocado, almonds, heating powder and 1/4 tsp salt in a bowl and mix to dispose of any bumps. Utilizing a hand whisk, mix the sugar into the softened chocolate blend, and beat well until smooth and sparkling, guaranteeing all the sugar is very much disintegrated. Mix from the flaxseed blend, vanilla concentrate, and chocolate, at that point the flour blend. Spoon into the readied tin.

3. Heat For 35-45 mins before a stick embedded into the middle tells the truth with wet morsels. Permit to cool in the tin totally, at that point cut into squares. Store in a sealed shut compartment and eat inside three events.

Asparagus and lemon with beans

Nourishment: each serving

kcal481

fat15g

saturates1g

carbs60g

sugars8g

fibre17g

protein19g

Salt0.04g

Ingredients

150g wholemeal spaghetti

160g asparagus, closes cut and cut into lengths

2 Tbsp rapeseed oil

2 leeks (220g), cut into lengths, at that point lean strips

1 red bean stew, deseeded and finely slashed

1 garlic clove, finely ground

160g Frozen peas

1 lemon, zested and squeezed, and wedges to serve

Plan

1. Heat up The spaghetti for 12 mins until still somewhat firm, Such as the asparagus for the last 3 mins. Then, heat the oil at a sizable skillet griddle, include the leeks and stew and stew for 5 mins. Mix in the peas, garlic and lemon pizzazz and squeeze and cook for a couple of mins more.

2. Channel And supplement the pasta to the container with 1/4 Mug of this pasta water and toss everything together until all around blended. Spoon into shallow dishes and present with lemon wedges for crushing over, on the off chance that you like.

CONCLUSION

Because of the colossal marketplace for effective health improvement strategies in our established social orders, there's become a torrential slip of varied get-healthy programs that were introduced to this gigantic sector.

Regardless, on the off chance that you research some of those projects, you may understand that"all the sparkles is not gold". Some of these things are really harmful to your health while some aren't as much as gainful since they promise to be.

This Way, in this Guide we will be exploring some bogus legends which encircle some of the eating regime and get-healthy plans which have hit the marketplace as of late:

- The primitive veggie lover diet Strategy

The advocates of the crude vegetarian diet program emotionally program folks into accepting this type of diet is helpful for their health while this eating regimen actually prompts genuine dietary and nutrient insufficiencies in case it isn't suitably improved.

Children who've tried this Sort of carefully primitive veggie enthusiast diet for important moves generated development problems such as the development of dangerously lower statures and body heaps in children, diminished bone depth and development of lean appendages.

A couple of kids profited from this Eating regimen also create bloated tummies and squeezed lips while a few other kids created rickets.

In case you have to be on this type of primitive eating regimen you should start looking for skilled exhortation and also you ought to boost this eating regimen together with the ideal steps of nutrient and healthful improvements.

- Meal substitution diet program

A real case of this sort of diet is your milder supper

substitution program which advocates you should limit your calorie entrance to 500 calories simply by supplanting your important dinners with lighter things such as shakes and soups. The weight watcher is advised to drink only water notwithstanding these products.

However, on the off chance that you do not stick to the guidelines within this eating regular arrangement industriously, it may prompt cataclysmic results; some individuals who drank a great deal of water in the aftermath of using the things within this eating regime program actually kicked the bucket.

In case you want to use this eating regime program, you must stick to the guidelines just.

- Acai berry organic Item

Among the most overhyped weight Reduction nourishments is acai berry; the larger portion of the publicizing attempts relating to this bogus super nutrition are brimming with bogus tributes and a whole lot of pseudo-science claims.

Some of the entertaining commercials concerning this organic product ensure it has purging and antimicrobial properties. Additionally, they guarantee that as soon as you're using this acai berry, then you do not need to change your eating regimen and lifestyle.

The fact of this situation is that in spite of the fact that acai berry includes a couple of minerals and nutrients, you may likewise receive a huge section of the nutritional supplements and nutrients it contains structure cheaper all-natural products such as lemons and oranges.

In addition in case that you consume only acai berry to get fit, each one of those pounds of fat that you lose will be regained as soon as you return to a regular eating regime; it induces real bounce back weight growth after you stop eating it.

- Hoodia diet pills

The diet pill is an ingestion Regular pill that's usually promoted as an urge suppressant that may trigger substantial weight loss. A couple of publicists of the pill also make a case for its aid of the pill by different names that are big.

Anyhow, reality with respect to This tablet is that the huge bulk of the logical preliminaries with this pill haven't given some indisputable and dependable positive effects accordingly discrediting the instances this tablet is a marvel weight reduction pill.

In Addition, You should Realize this Hoodia pill is yet to be wholly supported by the nutrition and medication organization referred to as the FDA. Along these lines, kindly do not eliminate control with the publicizing publicity about that particular pill.

- Excessive use of Nourishment

The medical Benefits of Nutrients are misrepresented to counterfeit elevated amounts recently and this has made many people incorrectly accept that using high levels of nourishment will make them grounded and raise their immune framework.

Anyhow in all actuality from the Event which you use exorbitantly significant doses of nutrients, it's possible to build up the corresponding intricacies:

A. If you consume over 1.5milligrams Of nutrient a of each daily that your bones will get feeble and more inclined to fractures.

B-If you expend over 1000mg Of vitamin C supplements within a day you are able to make looseness of the bowels and fart.

C-Excessive use of Nutrient A wealthy beta-carotene nourishments such as green lush vegetables, yellowish organic products such as mangoes, apricots and lemons really can build your probability of producing lung disorder especially in the event you are a smoker.

D-Consumption of past what 540 Milligrams of nutrient E may be damaging to your health.

E-Excessive use of more Than 0.3milligrams of selenium per day prompts phobias such as balding, nail obstruction and epidermis misfortune.

- Weight Stress teas and thinning cases

Many weight loss teas and thin cases have a compound called sibutramine which could result in real Hurtful ailments such as coronary strokes and episodes. In the event that you're keen on using weight-loss teas and weight reduction pills, you need to Assess their ingredients to make certain they don't include sibutramine.

Made in the USA
Coppell, TX
07 February 2020